Better Homes and Gardens
GROUND MEAT COOK BOOK

MEREDITH PRESS

NEW YORK   DES MOINES

CONTENTS

On the cover: Garden-fresh Stuffed Pepper Cups feature ground beef and rice. Scalloped edges add special effect.

Left: Drizzle cheese sauce laced with peas over Vegetable-Meat Cups. The potato filling is dotted with green onion.

Better Homes and Gardens TEST KITCHEN

Our seal assures you that every recipe in the *Ground Meat Cook Book* is endorsed by the Better Homes and Gardens Test Kitchen. Each recipe is tested for family appeal, practicality, and deliciousness.

EDITORIAL DIRECTOR: Don Dooley
MANAGING EDITOR: Malcolm E. Robinson   ART DIRECTOR: John Berg
SUPERVISING FOODS EDITOR: Nancy Morton
SENIOR FOODS EDITOR: Joyce Trollope
ASSOCIATE EDITOR: David Kastler
ASSISTANT EDITORS: Nancy Byal, Lorene Mundhenke, Janice McCord,
Sandra Wood, Sharyl Steffens
DESIGNERS: Julie Zesch, Ronald Garman, Arthur Riser, George Meininger

MEATS FOR FAMILY MEALS

Start spending less and enjoying it more—serve the family's favorite ground meat in a variety of ways. Whether it is ground beef, veal, pork, lamb, or ham, select a recipe from the following pages to whet the appetites of the family.

Put eye appeal in the meal with various meat shapes. Serve meat loaf, meatballs, or meat patties; or, offer stuffed peppers, tomatoes, cabbage rolls, or croquettes for a change of pace at mealtime.

Look for a new favorite for family dining among the numerous casseroles, meat pies, and skillet dishes— all featuring ground meat. And for the budget conscious, select recipes using ground leftover meats. These provide money-saving opportunities.

For a simple-to-prepare entree, serve the family Cherry-Sauced Ham Balls. Make the sauce with canned pie filling.

Shaping Meat Adds Mealtime Appeal

FAVORITE BEEF LOAF

No need to worry about leftovers with this one. If all the loaf is not eaten for dinner, it's perfect for cold sandwiches the next day—

     1 beef bouillon cube
    ½ cup boiling water
     1 beaten egg
    1½ cups soft bread crumbs
         (about 2 slices)
    ⅔ cup nonfat dry milk powder
    ¼ cup chopped onion
    ½ teaspoon salt
    ¼ teaspoon dried basil leaves,
         crushed
     1 pound ground beef

Dissolve bouillon cube in boiling water. Combine bouillon with egg, bread crumbs, dry milk powder, onion, salt, and basil. Add beef and mix well. Pat mixture into 7½x3¾x2¼-inch loaf pan, or shape into loaf in shallow baking dish. Bake meat loaf at 350° for 50 to 60 minutes. Makes 4 to 6 servings.

Stuffed Meat Loaf has a different twist. Not only is it made in a round dish, but it has a tasty layer of rice in the center.

TOMATO-BEEF LOAF

     1 beaten egg
    ⅓ cup milk
     1 8-ounce can tomatoes, cut up
    ½ cup quick-cooking rolled oats
     4 slices bacon, crisp-cooked and
         crumbled
    1½ teaspoons salt
     1 teaspoon Worcestershire sauce
     2 pounds ground beef

Combine first 7 ingredients and dash pepper. Add beef; mix well. Shape into 8x5-inch loaf in shallow baking pan. Bake at 350° for 1¼ hours. Makes 8 to 10 servings.

STUFFED MEAT LOAF

     2 beaten eggs
    ½ cup milk
    ⅓ cup fine dry bread crumbs
    ¼ cup finely chopped onion
     1 teaspoon salt
    ½ teaspoon ground sage
    1½ pounds ground beef
     1 beef bouillon cube
    ½ cup uncooked long-grain rice
    ¼ cup chopped onion
     2 tablespoons butter or margarine
     1 slightly beaten egg
    ½ teaspoon ground sage

Combine first 6 ingredients and dash pepper. Add beef; mix well. Dissolve bouillon cube in 1 cup boiling water. Cook rice in bouillon over low heat till liquid is absorbed, about 15 minutes. Cook onion in butter till tender but not brown. In bowl combine cooked rice, cooked onion, 1 slightly beaten egg, and ½ teaspoon sage. Pat *half* of meat mixture evenly in bottom of 8¼x1¾-inch round baking dish. Spread rice mixture over meat. Top with remaining meat. Bake at 350° for 50 minutes. Makes 6 to 8 servings.

FILLED BEEF ROLL

1 beaten egg
¼ cup milk
½ cup finely crushed saltine
cracker crumbs (14 crackers)
¼ cup chopped onion
½ teaspoon salt
Dash pepper
1 pound ground beef
1 cup cooked rice
2 ounces process Swiss cheese,
shredded (½ cup)
2 tablespoons chopped green pepper

Combine first 6 ingredients. Add beef; mix well. Pat mixture into a 10x8-inch rectangle on waxed paper. Combine cooked rice, cheese, and green pepper. Pat onto meat leaving 1 inch margin around edge. Roll jelly-roll fashion beginning with narrow side (see page 122). Seal side seam and ends. Place roll, seam side down, in 11x7x1½-inch baking pan. Bake at 350° for 35 minutes. Let stand 5 minutes before serving. Makes 4 or 5 servings.

MIDGET BEEF LOAVES

Combine 2 beaten eggs, one 10½-ounce can condensed onion soup, 1⅓ cups soft bread crumbs (2 slices), ¼ cup snipped parsley, 1 teaspoon Worcestershire sauce, and ¼ teaspoon salt. Add 2 pounds ground beef; mix well. Divide meat into 16 portions; pat into muffin pans. Bake at 350° for 25 to 30 minutes. Makes 8 servings.

MEXICAN MEAT LOAF

2 beaten eggs
1 8-ounce can tomatoes, cut up
½ cup fine dry bread crumbs
¼ cup finely chopped green pepper
1 tablespoon instant minced onion
1 to 2 teaspoons chili powder
1½ teaspoons salt
2 pounds ground beef

Combine first 7 ingredients. Add beef; mix well. Pat into 9x5x3-inch loaf pan. Bake at 350° for 1½ hours. Makes 8 to 10 servings.

For Swiss cheese fans, try the "jelly-roll meat loaf"—Filled Beef Roll. The filling teams rice, cheese, and green pepper.

BEEF AND APPLE LOAF

1 beaten egg
¼ cup milk
¾ cup soft bread crumbs
2 medium apples, peeled, cored,
and finely chopped (2 cups)
¼ cup chopped onion
1 teaspoon salt
⅛ teaspoon pepper
⅛ teaspoon ground nutmeg
1½ pounds ground beef

Combine egg, milk, crumbs, apple, onion, salt, pepper, and nutmeg. Add beef; mix well. Pat into 8½x4½x2½-inch loaf dish. Bake at 350° for 1¼ hours. Makes 6 servings.

INDIVIDUAL MEAT LOAVES

A quick way to bake meat loaf —

Combine 1 beaten egg, one 6-ounce can (⅔ cup) evaporated milk, ½ cup catsup, 1 cup soft bread crumbs, ⅓ cup chopped celery, ⅓ cup chopped onion, ⅓ cup chopped dill pickle, and 1 teaspoon salt. Add 2 pounds ground beef and mix well. Divide mixture into 16 portions; pat into muffin pans. Bake at 350° for 30 to 35 minutes. Makes 8 servings.

PEPPY-SAUCED MEAT LOAF

    1 beaten egg
    ⅛ cup milk
    1 tablespoon vinegar
    1 tablespoon molasses
    1 tablespoon prepared mustard
    1½ cups soft bread crumbs
        (about 2 slices)
    ¼ cup chopped onion
    ½ teaspoon salt
    1½ pounds ground beef
        Peppy Sauce

Combine egg, milk, vinegar, molasses, mustard, bread crumbs, onion, and salt. Add beef and mix well. Pat mixture into 8½x4½x2½-inch loaf dish. Bake at 350° for 1¼ hours.

Serve with *Peppy Sauce:* In saucepan combine one 10½-ounce can condensed beef broth, 2 teaspoons vinegar, 1 teaspoon prepared mustard, and 1 teaspoon molasses; beat till smooth. Blend together ½ cup cold water and 3 tablespoons all-purpose flour. Add to broth mixture. Cook and stir till thickened and bubbly. Makes 6 servings.

EVERYDAY MEAT LOAF

The catsup sauce makes a flavorful baked-on topper for any favorite meat loaf—

    2 beaten eggs
    ¾ cup milk
    ⅔ cup fine dry bread crumbs
    2 tablespoons grated onion
    1 teaspoon salt
    ½ teaspoon ground sage
        Dash pepper
    1½ pounds ground beef
            • • •
    ¼ cup catsup
    2 tablespoons brown sugar
    1 teaspoon dry mustard
    ¼ teaspoon ground nutmeg

Combine eggs, milk, bread crumbs, onion, salt, sage, and pepper. Add beef and mix well. Pat mixture into 8½x4½x2½-inch loaf dish. Bake at 350° for 1 hour. Combine remaining ingredients. Spread over meat loaf. Bake 15 minutes longer. Makes 6 servings.

ITALIAN MEAT LOAVES

    2 beaten eggs
    1 cup milk
    ¾ cup coarsely crushed saltine
        cracker crumbs (17 crackers)
    ½ cup grated Parmesan cheese
    ¼ cup finely chopped onion
    1 teaspoon Worcestershire sauce
    ½ teaspoon garlic salt
    ¼ teaspoon dried basil leaves,
        crushed
    1½ pounds ground beef
    3 tablespoons catsup

Combine first 8 ingredients and dash pepper. Add beef; mix well. Shape into 6 individual loaves. Place in shallow baking pan. Spread catsup over loaves. Sprinkle each with a little additional Parmesan cheese and crushed basil. Bake at 350° for 45 minutes. Serves 6.

SWEET-SOUR GLAZED LOAF

    2 beaten eggs
    ¼ cup chili sauce
    ½ cup crushed shredded wheat
        biscuit (1 large biscuit)
    ¼ cup chopped onion
    ½ teaspoon salt
    ¼ teaspoon dried marjoram
        leaves, crushed
    ⅛ teaspoon pepper
    1 pound ground beef
        Sweet-Sour Sauce

Combine eggs, chili sauce, shredded wheat, onion, salt, marjoram, and pepper. Add beef and mix well. Shape into a loaf in 11x7x1½-inch baking pan. Bake at 350° for 45 minutes.

Meanwhile, prepare *Sweet-Sour Sauce:* Drain one 8¾-ounce can pineapple tidbits, reserving syrup. Add enough water to syrup to make ¾ cup. Combine 2 tablespoons brown sugar and 1 tablespoon cornstarch in small saucepan. Stir in reserved syrup, 1 tablespoon vinegar, and 1 teaspoon soy sauce. Cook and stir till mixture thickens and bubbles. Stir in drained pineapple; heat to boiling.

Place meat loaf on serving platter. Spoon some sauce over top. Pass remaining sauce. Makes 4 or 5 servings.

Search for the Swiss cheese and ham surprise in the Hidden Treasure Loaf. Many markets feature a meat loaf mixture. Use this or mix one pound ground beef and half pound each of ground veal and ground pork. All beef is good too.

HIDDEN TREASURE LOAF

    2 beaten eggs
    ¼ cup milk
    ½ cup fine dry bread crumbs
    2 tablespoons snipped parsley
    1 tablespoon Worcestershire sauce
    1 teaspoon salt
    1 teaspoon monosodium glutamate
      Dash pepper
    2 pounds meat loaf mixture
    4 ounces process Swiss cheese,
        cubed (1 cup)
    4 ounces boiled ham, chopped
    1 tablespoon snipped parsley

Combine beaten eggs, milk, bread crumbs, 2 tablespoons parsley, Worcestershire sauce, salt, monosodium glutamate, and pepper. Add meat loaf mixture; mix well. Pat *two-thirds* of the meat mixture onto bottom and sides of lightly greased 9x5x3-inch loaf pan, forming a shell 1 inch thick.

Combine cubed cheese, ham, and 1 tablespoon parsley; spoon into meat shell. Top with remaining meat mixture; press edges to seal. Bake at 350° for 1¼ hours. Drain off excess fat; cool meat loaf in pan about 10 minutes. Loosen sides if necessary and turn out onto serving platter. Garnish meat loaf with curly endive, if desired. Serves 6 to 8.

What could be easier than a meat loaf for dinner! Mushroom-Sauced Loaf makes the perfect main dish for an oven meal. Accompany it with baked potatoes, carrots, and a crisp green salad. For dessert, serve baked apples. Another speedy sauce that would be good with the meat loaf is **Quick Mushroom Sauce:** Stir 1 cup dairy sour cream into one 10½-ounce can condensed cream of mushroom soup; heat.

MUSHROOM-SAUCED LOAF

    1 beaten egg
    ⅓ cup milk
    ⅓ cup fine dry bread crumbs
    3 tablespoons finely chopped
        green onion
    3 tablespoons snipped parsley
    ¾ teaspoon salt
    ¾ teaspoon Worcestershire sauce
    ⅛ teaspoon ground nutmeg
        Dash pepper
    1½ pounds ground beef
        Mushroom Sauce

Combine the first 9 ingredients. Add beef and mix well. Pat mixture into 8½x4½x2½-inch loaf dish. Bake at 350° for 1¼ hours.

Meanwhile, prepare *Mushroom Sauce:* Drain one 6-ounce can sliced mushrooms. In saucepan melt 3 tablespoons butter or margarine. Stir in 1 tablespoon all-purpose flour, dash salt, and dash pepper. Add ¾ cup milk all at once. Cook and stir till mixture thickens and bubbles. Add mushrooms; heat through. Serve with meat loaf. Makes 6 servings.

BEEF AND SAUSAGE LOAF

Sausage and tomato juice add a special juiciness and flavor to this meat loaf—

    ½ cup chopped onion
    2 tablespoons chopped green pepper
    2 tablespoons butter or margarine
            • • •
    2 beaten eggs
    ⅓ cup tomato juice
    ½ cup quick-cooking rolled oats
    1 teaspoon salt
    ¼ teaspoon dry mustard
    1½ pounds ground beef
    ½ pound bulk pork sausage

Cook onion and green pepper in butter till tender but not brown. Combine eggs with next 4 ingredients and cooked vegetables. Add beef and sausage and mix well. Pat mixture into 8½x4½x2½-inch loaf dish. Bake at 350° for 1½ hours. Remove from oven and pour off excess fat. Let meat stand in pan several minutes before slicing. Makes 8 servings.

OLIVE MEAT LOAF

    ¾ cup milk
    1 cup packaged herb-seasoned
        stuffing mix
    2 beaten eggs
    ½ cup sliced pimiento-stuffed
        green olives
    2 tablespoons finely chopped onion
    1 teaspoon salt
        Dash pepper
    1½ pounds ground beef
    ½ pound bulk pork sausage

Pour milk over stuffing mix; set aside till milk is absorbed. Combine eggs, olives, onion, salt, and pepper. Add beef and sausage; mix well. Add stuffing mixture and mix thoroughly. Pat into 9x5x3-inch loaf pan. Bake at 350° for 1½ hours. Makes 6 to 8 servings.

MEAT LOAF SWIRL

A meat loaf within a meat loaf—

    1 beaten egg
    ½ cup milk
    ¼ cup chopped onion
    2 teaspoons salt
        Dash pepper
    2 pounds ground beef
    1 beaten egg
    1½ cups soft bread crumbs
        (about 2 slices)
    1½ cups shredded raw potato
    ¼ cup chopped onion
    2 tablespoons snipped parsley
    1 teaspoon ground sage
    ½ teaspoon salt
    ½ pound ground pork

Combine 1 egg, milk, ¼ cup chopped onion, 2 teaspoons salt, and dash pepper. Add beef; mix well. On waxed paper, pat beef mixture to a 10-inch square; set aside.

Combine 1 egg, bread crumbs, potato, ¼ cup chopped onion, parsley, sage, and ½ teaspoon salt. Add pork and mix well. Spread over beef layer. Roll up jelly-roll fashion (see page 122). Place seam side down in shallow baking pan. Bake at 350° for 1¼ hours. Makes 8 to 10 servings.

CARAWAY MEAT LOAF

  1 tablespoon instant minced onion
  2 teaspoons caraway seed
  3 tablespoons red wine vinegar
  1 beaten egg
  ¼ cup milk
1½ cups soft bread crumbs
    (about 2 slices)
  1 teaspoon salt
    Dash pepper
  1 pound ground beef
  ½ pound ground pork
  ½ cup dairy sour cream
  1 tablespoon all-purpose flour
  1 beef bouillon cube
  ½ cup boiling water

Soak onion and caraway seed in vinegar for 10 minutes. Combine egg, milk, vinegar mixture, crumbs, salt, and pepper. Add beef and pork; mix well. Shape in 8x4-inch loaf in shallow baking pan. Bake at 350° for 1¼ hours.

    Serve with Sour Cream Sauce: In small saucepan blend together sour cream and flour. Dissolve bouillon cube in boiling water; gradually stir into sour cream. Cook and stir over medium-low heat till thickened and bubbly. Cook and stir 1 minute more. Serves 6.

SAUSAGE-LIVER LOAF

  1 pound calves liver
  1 small onion, quartered
  2 beaten eggs
  ⅓ cup milk
  ¼ cup catsup
1½ cups soft bread crumbs
    (about 2 slices)
  1 teaspoon Worcestershire sauce
  ¼ teaspoon salt
    Dash pepper
  1 pound bulk pork sausage

Cover liver with water; bring to boil and simmer 5 minutes. Drain; put liver and onion through food grinder using medium blade. Combine remaining ingredients. Add liver and onion; mix thoroughly. Pat into 8½x 4½x2½-inch loaf dish. Bake at 350° for 1½ hours. Unmold. Serve with additional catsup, if desired. Makes 8 to 10 servings.

TOP-NOTCH TURKEY LOAF

  2 beaten eggs
  1 6-ounce can evaporated milk
  ⅓ cup chicken broth
1½ cups soft bread crumbs
    (about 2 slices)
  ⅔ cup finely chopped celery
  ¾ teaspoon salt
    Dash pepper
    Dash ground nutmeg
    Dash dried rosemary leaves,
      crushed
    Dash dried marjoram leaves,
      crushed
  4 cups coarsely ground cooked
    turkey
  1 10½-ounce can condensed cream
    of chicken soup
  ⅓ cup milk
  2 tablespoons chopped canned
    pimiento

Combine eggs, milk, broth, bread crumbs, celery, and seasonings. Add turkey and mix well. Line bottom of greased 8½x4½x2½-inch loaf dish with foil; grease foil. Pat in turkey mixture. Bake at 350° for 45 minutes, till center of loaf is firm. Invert onto serving platter; remove foil. Serve with Pimiento Sauce: Heat together chicken soup, milk, and pimiento. Makes 6 servings.

LAMB LOAF WITH OLIVES

  2 beaten eggs
  ⅓ cup milk
1½ cups soft bread crumbs
    (about 2 slices)
  ½ cup thinly sliced pimiento-
    stuffed green olives
  ¼ cup finely chopped celery
  ¼ cup finely chopped onion
  1 teaspoon salt
  ¼ teaspoon dried oregano leaves,
    crushed
  2 pounds ground lamb

Combine eggs, milk, crumbs, olives, celery, onion, salt, and oregano. Add lamb and mix thoroughly. Pat into 9x5x3-inch loaf pan. Bake at 350° for 1½ hours. Serves 8.

Looking for a way to use those leftover holiday turkey pieces? Present Top-Notch Turkey Loaf to the family. If desired, ground cooked chicken can be substituted for the turkey. Dashes of spices and herbs add flavor to the loaf as does the chopped celery scattered throughout. To make the loaf a bit special, serve the jiffy pimiento sauce atop. Just start with a can of cream of chicken soup and add milk and pimiento. Presto—a colorful and delicious addition to the flavorful loaf.

CHILI LOAF

- 2 beaten eggs
- 1 8-ounce can tomatoes, cut up
- 1 8-ounce can kidney beans, drained
- ½ cup fine dry bread crumbs
- ¼ cup chopped onion
- 2 tablespoons snipped parsley
- 1½ teaspoons salt
- ½ to 1 teaspoon chili powder
- 1 pound ground beef
- 1 pound ground veal

Combine first 8 ingredients; add beef and veal. Mix well, mashing up beans slightly. Pat mixture into 9x5x3-inch loaf pan. Bake at 350° for 1½ hours. Serves 8 to 10.

VEAL LOAF

Combine 1 beaten egg; ½ cup milk; ½ cup finely crushed saltine cracker crumbs (14 crackers); ½ cup shredded carrot; ¼ cup chopped onion; ¼ cup chopped celery; 2 tablespoons chili sauce; ½ teaspoon salt; and dash pepper. Add 1½ pounds ground veal; mix well. Shape into a loaf on shallow baking pan. Bake at 350° for 1 hour. Serves 6.

VEGETABLE MEAT LOAF

- ½ cup chopped celery
- 2 tablespoons butter or margarine
- 1 beaten egg
- 2 medium tomatoes, peeled and finely chopped (1⅓ cups)
- 1½ cups soft bread crumbs (about 2 slices)
- ½ cup chopped green onion
- ¼ cup snipped parsley
- 1½ teaspoons salt
- 1½ pounds ground beef
- 1 pound ground veal

Cook celery in butter till tender but not brown. Combine egg, tomatoes, crumbs, green onion, cooked celery, parsley, and salt. Add beef and veal; mix well. Pat mixture into 9x5x3-inch loaf pan. Bake at 350° for 1¾ hours or till done. Makes 10 servings.

APRICOT-TOPPED LOAF

- 2 beaten eggs
- ½ cup fine dry bread crumbs
- ¼ cup chopped green onion
- ¾ teaspoon salt
- 1 pound ground veal
- 1 pound bulk pork sausage
- ½ cup snipped dried apricots
- 1 cup water
- ½ cup brown sugar
- ⅛ teaspoon ground cloves
- 1 tablespoon cornstarch

Combine eggs, bread crumbs, green onion, and salt; add veal and sausage and mix well. Shape into 7x4½-inch loaf on shallow baking pan. Bake at 350° for 1¼ hours. Meanwhile, combine apricots, water, brown sugar, and cloves in saucepan. Simmer, covered, for 20 minutes or till apricots are tender. Mix cornstarch with ¼ cup cold water. Add to sauce. Cook and stir 2 minutes longer or till bubbly. Serve with meat loaf. Makes 8 to 10 servings.

SAUSAGE SCRAPPLE

- 2 pounds bulk pork sausage
- 1 14½-ounce can (1⅔ cups) evaporated milk
- 3 cups water
- 1½ cups yellow cornmeal
- ½ teaspoon salt
- All-purpose flour *or* cornflake crumbs
- 2 beaten eggs
- 3 to 4 tablespoons shortening

Brown sausage slowly breaking it up into small pieces; drain off excess fat. Combine milk and water. Add 4 cups of the milk mixture to sausage. Reserve remaining milk mixture. Heat sausage mixture to boiling; slowly stir in cornmeal and salt. Cook 5 minutes, stirring constantly. Pour into greased 9x5x3-inch loaf pan. Chill till firm.

Unmold and cut into ¼-inch slices. Dip in flour *or* cornflake crumbs. Combine eggs and remaining milk mixture. Dip slices in egg mixture then in flour or crumbs again. In skillet brown in hot shortening on both sides. Serve hot with warm syrup. Serves 10 to 12.

SWEET-SOUR HAM LOAF

    ½ cup brown sugar
    ¼ cup vinegar
    2 tablespoons prepared mustard
    2 beaten eggs
    ½ cup milk
    ½ cup coarsely crushed saltine
        cracker crumbs (11 crackers)
      Dash pepper
    1½ pounds ground fully-cooked ham
    ½ pound ground pork

Blend brown sugar, vinegar, and mustard; set aside. Combine eggs, milk, crumbs, and pepper. Add ham and pork; mix well. Add *half* the brown sugar mixture; mix well. Shape into a loaf in 10x6x1½-inch baking dish. Pour remaining brown sugar mixture over loaf. Bake at 350° for 1¼ hours. Serves 6 to 8.

UPSIDE-DOWN HAM LOAF

    2 beaten eggs
    ½ cup milk
    1½ cups soft bread crumbs
        (about 2 slices)
    1 teaspoon salt
    ½ teaspoon poultry seasoning
    ¼ teaspoon pepper
    1 pound ground beef
    1 pound ground fully-cooked ham
    1 8¾-ounce can pineapple tidbits
    ¼ cup brown sugar
    2 teaspoons prepared mustard
    1 teaspoon cornstarch

Combine eggs, milk, crumbs, and seasonings. Add meats and mix well. Drain pineapple reserving 2 tablespoons syrup. Arrange pineapple tidbits on bottom of 9x5x3-inch loaf pan. Carefully pat meat mixture on top of pineapple. Bake at 350° for 1½ hours.

Drain off pan juices and reserve. Turn loaf out upside down onto platter. Skim excess fat from pan juices. In saucepan combine pan juices with brown sugar, reserved pineapple syrup, and mustard. Blend cornstarch and 1 tablespoon cold water; add to brown sugar mixture. Cook and stir till mixture thickens and bubbles. Cook 1 minute longer. Spoon over loaf. Makes 8 servings.

HAM LOAF

    1 10¾-ounce can condensed
        tomato soup
    1 beaten egg
    ⅓ cup milk
    ¾ cup coarsely crushed saltine
        cracker crumbs (17 crackers)
    ⅓ cup chopped onion
    1 pound ground fully-cooked ham
    1 pound ground beef
      Mustard Sauce

Reserve *half* the soup for sauce. Combine remaining soup, egg, milk, crumbs, and onion. Add ham and beef; mix well. Pat mixture into 9x5x3-inch loaf pan. Bake at 350° for 1½ hours. Drain off excess fat. Let stand 5 minutes, then turn out on platter.

Serve with *Mustard Sauce:* Mix reserved soup with 1 beaten egg; 1 tablespoon sugar; 2 tablespoons prepared mustard; 1 tablespoon vinegar; and 1 tablespoon butter or margarine, melted. Cook, stirring constantly, just till mixture bubbles. Makes 8 servings.

Mustard Sauce zips up this luscious Ham Loaf. It is not the typically yellow mustard-type sauce—it starts with tomato soup. The perfect vegetable partner is buttery parslied new potatoes.

HAM-RICE LOAVES

⅓ cup uncooked long-grain rice
2 beaten eggs
¾ cup milk
½ cup finely chopped onion
½ teaspoon salt
Dash pepper
1 pound ground fully-cooked ham
(3 cups)
1 pound ground veal
Paprika
1 tablespoon instant minced onion
¼ cup milk
1 cup dairy sour cream
2 tablespoons prepared mustard

Cook rice according to package directions. Combine eggs, ¾ cup milk, cooked rice, chopped onion, salt, and pepper. Add ham and veal; mix well. Pat mixture into six 4½x 2¾x2¼-inch loaf pans *or* one 9x5x3-inch loaf pan. Sprinkle with paprika. Bake at 350° for 40 to 45 minutes for small loaves or 1½ hours for large loaf.

Serve with Mustard Sauce: Soften instant minced onion in ¼ cup milk. In a small saucepan stir onion and milk into the sour cream. Add prepared mustard. Heat and stir over low heat (do not boil). Makes 6 servings.

Ham-Rice Loaves are individual meat loaves that not only bake faster than a large loaf, but make attractive servings.

BUTTERMILK-HAM LOAF

1 beaten egg
1½ cups buttermilk
½ cup fine dry bread crumbs
¼ teaspoon ground cinnamon
(optional)
1 pound ground fully-cooked ham
1 pound ground pork

Combine egg, buttermilk, crumbs, and cinnamon. Add ham and pork; mix well. Pat mixture into 9x5x3-inch loaf pan. Bake at 350° for 1½ hours. Makes 8 servings.

ZIPPY-TOPPED HAM LOAF

2 beaten eggs
1 cup milk
¾ cup coarsely crushed saltine
cracker crumbs (17 crackers)
2 pounds ground fully-cooked ham
1 pound ground pork
Horseradish Sauce

Combine eggs, milk, and crumbs. Add ham and pork; mix well. Pat mixture into 9x9x2-inch baking pan. Bake at 350° for 1¼ hours. Cut into squares and serve with *Horseradish Sauce:* Whip 1 cup whipping cream till peaks begin to form. Fold in 2 tablespoons prepared horseradish, 2 teaspoons sugar, and 1 teaspoon lemon juice. Makes 12 servings.

APRICOT-HAM SQUARES

2 beaten eggs
1 22-ounce can apricot pie filling
2½ cups soft bread crumbs
2 tablespoons chopped onion
1 tablespoon chopped green pepper
1 pound ground fully-cooked ham
1 pound ground beef

Combine eggs, *1 cup* of the pie filling, crumbs, onion, green pepper, and dash pepper. Add ham and beef; mix well. Pat into 8x8x2-inch baking dish. Bake at 350° for 30 minutes. Spread remaining pie filling over top. Bake 15 minutes longer. Spoon off excess meat juices. Cut into squares. Makes 8 servings.

SALISBURY STEAK

    1 beaten egg
    ½ cup soft bread crumbs
    ¼ cup finely chopped onion
    2 tablespoons finely chopped green
       pepper
1½ teaspoons salt
    ¼ teaspoon pepper
    2 pounds ground beef

Combine first 6 ingredients; add beef and mix well. Shape into 6 patties, ¾ inch thick. Broil 3 inches from heat for 6 minutes. Turn and broil 4 minutes longer. Makes 6 servings.

CHICKEN-FRIED BURGERS

1½ pounds ground beef
    ¼ cup finely chopped onion
    ½ teaspoon salt
    ⅛ teaspoon pepper
    1 beaten egg
    1 2⅜-ounce package seasoned
       coating mix for chicken
      Shortening

Combine beef, onion, salt, and pepper; mix well. Shape into 6 patties. Dip patties in beaten egg, then in coating mix. Slowly brown on both sides in small amount of hot shortening, about 15 minutes. Makes 6 servings.

RED FLANNEL BURGERS

    2 beaten eggs
    2 tablespoons chopped onion
    1 teaspoon salt
      Dash pepper
    1 pound ground beef
    1 medium potato, cooked, peeled,
       and diced (1 cup)
    ½ cup finely diced pickled beets
    2 tablespoons shortening

Combine first 4 ingredients in bowl. Add beef and mix well. Add potatoes and beets; mix lightly. Chill thoroughly, about 1 hour. Shape into 8 patties, ¾ inch thick. Panfry patties in hot shortening 5 minutes; turn and cook 5 minutes longer. Makes 4 servings.

SAUSAGE AND APPLE RINGS

    1 pound bulk pork sausage
    1 slightly beaten egg
    ¾ cup finely crushed saltine
       cracker crumbs (21 crackers)
    2 tablespoons salad oil

         · · ·

    2 medium unpeeled red apples,
       cored and cut in ½-inch rings
    1 cup cranberry juice cocktail
    1 tablespoon cornstarch
    2 teaspoons sugar
    2 tablespoons cold water

Shape sausage into 4 patties, about ½ inch thick. Dip patties into egg, then into cracker crumbs. In skillet cook patties slowly on both sides in hot oil till brown, about 20 minutes; drain off excess fat.

    Meanwhile, in another skillet place apple rings in cranberry juice cocktail; simmer just till tender, 5 to 8 minutes. Remove apple rings. Blend cornstarch with sugar; stir in water. Add to cranberry juice and cook, stirring constantly, till juice thickens and bubbles. Return apple rings to sauce; heat through. To serve, top sausage patties with apple rings and spoon some sauce over. Garnish with parsley, if desired. Makes 4 servings.

SWEET-SOUR PATTIES

    Combine ¼ cup milk; 1 cup soft bread crumbs (about 1½ slices); 1 teaspoon salt; ⅛ teaspoon ground nutmeg; and ⅛ teaspoon dried thyme leaves, crushed. Add 1 pound ground beef; mix well. Shape into 4 patties.

    In medium skillet cook 1 onion, sliced, in 2 tablespoons butter or margarine till tender but not brown. Remove from skillet. Brown meat patties in same skillet. Return onions to skillet with browned meat patties.

    Combine ¼ cup vinegar, 2 tablespoons brown sugar, 2 tablespoons water, and ½ teaspoon dry mustard. Pour over meat and onions in skillet. Cover and simmer 35 minutes. Remove patties to serving dish. Skim fat from broth. Blend together 1 teaspoon cornstarch and 1 tablespoon cold water. Add to broth; cook and stir till thickened and bubbly. Serve over patties. Serves 4.

BEAN AND CHEESE PATTIES

2 beaten eggs
¼ cup catsup
¼ cup finely crushed saltine
  cracker crumbs (7 crackers)
2 tablespoons chopped onion
2 teaspoons Worcestershire sauce
1 pound ground beef
1 tablespoon salad oil
1 10½-ounce can condensed cream
  of mushroom soup
1 16-ounce can kidney beans
⅓ cup chopped green pepper
4 ounces sharp process American
  cheese, shredded (1 cup)

Mix first 5 ingredients, ¼ teaspoon salt, and dash pepper. Add beef; mix well. Shape into 4 or 5 patties. Brown in hot oil; spoon soup over. Drain beans; sprinkle vegetables and cheese atop patties. Cook slowly, covered, 10 to 15 minutes. Serves 4 or 5.

ROAST BEEF PATTIES

¼ cup chopped onion
3 tablespoons butter or margarine
¼ cup all-purpose flour
½ cup milk
2 cups ground cooked roast beef
2 tablespoons snipped parsley
1 tablespoon chili sauce
1 beaten egg
⅓ cup fine dry bread crumbs
2 tablespoons butter or margarine
  Mushroom Sauce

Cook onion in 3 tablespoons butter; blend in flour. Add milk; cook and stir till bubbly. Remove from heat. Blend in beef, parsley, chili sauce, and ¼ teaspoon salt. Chill.

Shape into 6 to 8 patties. Mix egg with 2 tablespoons water. Dip patties in egg, then in crumbs. Brown in 2 tablespoons butter.

Serve with *Mushroom Sauce:* Cook ¼ cup chopped onion and ¼ cup chopped green pepper in 1 tablespoon butter till tender. Add one 10½-ounce can condensed cream of mushroom soup; one 3-ounce can chopped mushrooms, drained and finely chopped; ⅓ cup milk; and dash pepper. Heat. Serves 4.

PIZZA WHEELS

1 beaten egg
⅓ cup milk
⅓ cup fine dry bread crumbs
⅓ cup finely chopped onion
2 pounds ground beef
1 8-ounce can tomato sauce
1 3-ounce can chopped mushrooms,
  drained and finely chopped
¾ teaspoon dried basil leaves,
  crushed
3 slices mozzarella cheese, cut
  in strips

Combine first 4 ingredients and ¾ teaspoon salt. Add meat; mix well. In shallow baking pan shape into 7 or 8 circles, about 4- to 4½-inches in diameter building a 1-inch-high edge. Combine tomato sauce, mushrooms, and basil; spoon into patties. Bake at 375° for 30 minutes. Lay cheese spoke-fashion atop pizzas. Bake 2 minutes. Serves 7 or 8.

BLUE CHEESE-SAUCED LOGS

1 beaten egg
2 tablespoons milk
¾ cup soft bread crumbs
¼ cup snipped parsley
1 tablespoon prepared mustard
1 pound ground beef *or* ground veal
2 tablespoons shortening
1 10½-ounce can condensed cream
  of chicken soup
¾ cup milk
1 ounce blue cheese, crumbled
  (¼ cup)

Combine first 5 ingredients and ¼ teaspoon salt. Add meat; mix well. Shape into eight 4x1-inch logs. In skillet brown logs on all sides in hot shortening. Blend remaining ingredients; pour over logs. Simmer, covered, 20 to 25 minutes. To serve, drizzle some sauce over meat; pass remaining. Serves 4.

Flavor-packed Pizza Wheels are certain→ to turn the heads of teen-age pizza fans. Individual servings make this entree easy to serve either in or out of doors.

Spoon canned cranberry sauce atop individual loaves of beef and sausage for colorful Cranberry-Glazed Loaves.

CRANBERRY-GLAZED LOAVES

　　1　beaten egg
　⅓　cup milk
　⅓　cup quick-cooking rolled oats
　　2　tablespoons finely chopped onion
　½　teaspoon salt
　　　Dash pepper
　　1　pound ground beef
　¼　pound bulk pork sausage
　½　16-ounce can whole cranberry
　　　　sauce (1 cup)
　¼　cup brown sugar
　　2　teaspoons lemon juice

Combine first 6 ingredients; add beef and sausage and mix well. Shape into 5 individual loaves. Place loaves in 13x9x2-inch baking dish or pan. Combine cranberry sauce, brown sugar, and lemon juice; spoon over loaves. Bake at 350° for 45 minutes. Serves 5.

SAUSAGE STACK-UPS

　¼　cup milk
　¼　cup fine dry bread crumbs
　　2　tablespoons finely chopped onion
　½　pound bulk pork sausage
　　2　cups packaged biscuit mix
　　　Onion Gravy

Combine first 3 ingredients; add sausage and mix well. Shape into 6 patties each 3 inches in diameter. Brown slowly; set aside. Reserve 2 tablespoons pan drippings. Prepare biscuit mix following package directions for biscuits. Roll to 12x10-inch rectangle on floured surface. Cut into twelve 3-inch rounds. Place 6 biscuits on ungreased baking sheet; top each with meat patty, then second biscuit. Bake at 400° for 15 minutes.

Top with *Onion Gravy:* Cook ¼ cup finely chopped onion in reserved pan drippings till tender but not brown. (If necessary, add butter or margarine to make 2 tablespoons.) Add 2 tablespoons all-purpose flour, ¾ teaspoon salt, ¼ teaspoon paprika, and dash pepper. Stir in 1½ cups milk all at once. Cook and stir till thick and bubbly. Serves 3 or 4.

STUFFED SAUSAGE PATTIES

Use stuffing mix to add convenience to this flavorful entree topped with a spiced crab apple—

　1½　pounds bulk pork sausage
　　1　cup packaged herb-seasoned
　　　　stuffing mix
　　2　tablespoons butter or margarine
　　1　cup finely chopped, peeled
　　　　tart apple
　½　cup finely chopped celery
　¼　cup finely chopped onion
　¼　cup snipped parsley
　　2　tablespoons chili sauce
　¼　teaspoon dry mustard
　　6　spiced crab apples

Shape sausage in 12 thin patties, ¼ inch thick. *Using ¼ cup water and 2 tablespoons butter or margarine*, prepare stuffing mix following package directions. Add chopped apple, celery, onion, parsley, chili sauce, and dry mustard; toss together lightly to mix.

Arrange 6 sausage patties in 13x9x2-inch pan. Top each patty with ½ cup stuffing mixture, then with another patty. Secure patties with wooden picks through center. Bake at 375° for 45 minutes or till done. Top each with a spiced crab apple. Makes 6 servings.

PINEAPPLE-VEAL PATTIES

  1 8½-ounce can sliced pineapple
      (4 slices)
  2 beaten eggs
  ¼ cup fine dry bread crumbs
      (about 1 slice)
  ¼ cup catsup
  2 tablespoons finely chopped onion
  ½ teaspoon salt
  ⅛ teaspoon dried thyme leaves,
      crushed
  2 cups ground cooked roast veal
      (½ pound)
  2 tablespoons shortening
  2 tablespoons brown sugar
  2 tablespoons butter or margarine,
      melted

Drain pineapple reserving ¼ cup syrup. Combine eggs with next 5 ingredients; add veal and mix well. Shape into 4 large patties. Brown patties in hot shortening. Remove from skillet. In same skillet combine reserved syrup, brown sugar, and butter. Arrange pineapple slices in mixture; top with patties. Cover; simmer 10 minutes. Remove to platter. Spoon syrup mixture over. Serves 4.

TURKEY TIMBALES

  2 beaten eggs
  1 cup milk
  ½ cup quick-cooking rolled oats
  1 cup chopped celery
  1 tablespoon finely chopped onion
  ½ teaspoon salt
  ¼ teaspoon dried rosemary leaves,
      crushed
      Dash pepper
  2 cups ground cooked turkey
  1 10½-ounce can condensed cream
      of mushroom soup
  ⅓ cup milk

Combine first 8 ingredients; add turkey and mix well. Pour into 4 greased 6-ounce custard cups. Bake at 350° for 45 to 50 minutes. Run spatula around timbales. Let stand 5 minutes before removing from cups. Combine mushroom soup and ⅓ cup milk in saucepan. Heat. Serve with timbales. Makes 4 servings.

POLISH CUTLETS

  ¼ cup milk
  ¼ cup butter or margarine, melted
  1 cup soft bread crumbs
      (about 1½ slices)
  ½ teaspoon lemon juice
  ½ teaspoon paprika
  ½ teaspoon salt
1½ pounds ground veal
  1 beaten egg
  ½ cup fine dry bread crumbs
  2 tablespoons shortening
      Gravy

Combine first 6 ingredients and dash pepper; add veal and mix well. Form into 6 patties, ¾ inch thick. Combine egg with 2 tablespoons water; dip patties into egg mixture, then into dry bread crumbs. In skillet brown patties on both sides in hot shortening. Simmer, covered, for 15 to 20 minutes.

To prepare *Gravy:* Remove patties to warm platter. Pour off pan drippings reserving 1 tablespoon. To reserved drippings in skillet, blend in 1 tablespoon all-purpose flour, ¼ teaspoon ground nutmeg, ¼ teaspoon salt, and dash pepper. Add 1 cup milk all at once. Cook, stirring constantly, till mixture thickens and bubbles. Stir in 1 teaspoon lemon juice. Serve with patties. Makes 6 servings.

GINGERED LAMB PATTIES

  1 beaten egg
  ½ cup finely crushed gingersnap
      crumbs (8 gingersnaps)
  ¾ teaspoon salt
      Dash pepper
  1 pound ground lamb
  ½ cup catsup
  2 tablespoons brown sugar
  ½ teaspoon dry mustard

Combine egg, gingersnaps, salt, and pepper. Add lamb and mix well. Form into 4 patties, about ¾ inch thick. Combine remaining ingredients for sauce. Broil patties 3 to 4 inches from heat 5 minutes; brush with sauce. Broil 3 minutes longer; turn. Broil 4 minutes; brush with sauce. Broil 3 minutes longer or till done. Makes 4 servings.

HAM PATTIES

Combine 1 beaten egg, ⅓ cup milk, ½ cup soft bread crumbs, ¼ cup chopped green onion, dash pepper, and 2 cups ground fully-cooked ham. Shape into 4 patties. Brown in small amount hot shortening. Heat and stir 1 cup dairy sour cream till hot. Spoon atop patties; top with snipped green onion. Serves 4.

FRUITED HAM CROQUETTES

½ cup sifted all-purpose flour
1 teaspoon baking powder
¼ teaspoon ground nutmeg
¼ teaspoon ground cinnamon
1 slightly beaten egg
1 8¾-ounce can crushed
    pineapple, *well* drained
1½ cups ground fully-cooked ham
    Fat for frying

Sift together dry ingredients. Add egg and *well*-drained pineapple; mix well. Fold in ham. Drop by tablespoonfuls into deep hot fat (365°). Fry 1 minute or till deep golden brown on all sides. Drain. Serve with warm syrup, if desired. Makes 15 croquettes.

Fill fryer only half full of fat to avoid spills and spatters. Fry small quantities of food at one time for even cooking.

HAM AND POTATO PATTIES

A good way to use leftovers after the holidays—

2 cups ground fully-cooked ham
1 cup leftover mashed potatoes
2 tablespoons chopped onion
2 teaspoons prepared mustard
    Dash pepper
1 beaten egg
1 tablespoon milk
½ cup fine dry bread crumbs
3 to 4 tablespoons salad oil
1 10-ounce package peas and
    cream sauce

Combine ham, potatoes, onion, mustard, and pepper. Shape into 12 patties. Blend egg with milk. Dip patties in egg mixture, then in crumbs. Fry in hot oil till golden brown. Heat peas and cream sauce following package directions. Serve atop patties. Makes 6 servings.

HAM AND RICE CROQUETTES

1 pound ground fully-cooked ham
    (3 cups)
1 10½-ounce can condensed cream
    of celery soup
1 cup cooked rice
1 tablespoon finely chopped onion
1 tablespoon finely chopped green
    pepper
1 to 2 tablespoons prepared
    mustard
1 beaten egg
1 cup fine dry bread crumbs
    Fat for frying
    Creamy Egg Sauce

Combine first 6 ingredients; mix well. Chill. Shape into cones, using about ¼ cup mixture per cone. Dip in egg, then in crumbs; let stand a few minutes. Fry 2 or 3 in deep hot fat (365°) for 3 to 5 minutes or till brown. Drain. Repeat with remaining croquettes.

Serve with *Creamy Egg Sauce:* Melt ¼ cup butter or margarine; blend in ¼ cup all-purpose flour, ½ teaspoon salt, and dash white pepper. Add 2 cups milk all at once. Cook and stir till thickened and bubbly. Add 2 hard-cooked eggs, chopped. Serves 8 to 10.

LAMB WITH DILL SAUCE

Combine 1 beaten egg; ½ cup quick-cooking rolled oats; ¼ cup finely chopped onion; 1 teaspoon salt; ¼ teaspoon dried thyme leaves, crushed; and dash pepper. Add 1½ pounds ground lamb and mix well. Shape mixture into 6 patties. Using 6 slices bacon, wrap each patty with 1 slice bacon; secure with wooden pick. Broil 5 inches from heat for 10 minutes. Turn; broil 5 minutes more. Serve with Dill Sauce. Makes 6 servings.

Dill Sauce: Cook 1 tablespoon finely chopped onion in 1 tablespoon butter or margarine till tender. Blend in 2 teaspoons all-purpose flour, 2 tablespoons grated Parmesan cheese, ½ teaspoon dried dillweed, ½ teaspoon paprika, and dash salt. Add 1 cup milk all at once. Cook, stirring constantly, till mixture is thickened and bubbly.

DEVILED LAMBURGERS

    1 tablespoon prepared mustard
    ½ teaspoon garlic salt
    ¼ teaspoon dried thyme leaves,
        crushed
    1 pound ground lamb
    1 tablespoon shortening
    4 thin slices onion
    4 green pepper rings
    4 thin slices lemon

Combine first 3 ingredients and dash pepper; add lamb and mix well. Shape into 4 patties. In skillet brown patties in hot shortening; drain. Top each burger with onion slice. Add 2 tablespoons water; cover and simmer for 10 minutes. Top each burger with green pepper ring and lemon slice; cook, covered, 10 to 15 minutes more or till done. Serves 4.

Delight lamb lovers by serving Lamb with Dill Sauce. Dill and Parmesan cheese combine in the creamy sauce spooned atop bacon-wrapped lamb patties.

FRANK AND BEEF ROLLS

1 beaten egg
¼ cup milk
1½ cups soft bread crumbs
2 tablespoons finely chopped onion
1 pound ground beef
4 frankfurters *or* fully-cooked
    smoked sausage links
    Dijon-style mustard
2 tablespoons all-purpose flour
2 tablespoons shortening
    Gravy

Combine first 4 ingredients, ½ teaspoon salt, and dash pepper. Add beef; mix well. Divide into 8 portions. Cut franks crosswise; spread generously with mustard. Shape meat around franks to form rolls, leaving ends of franks exposed. Coat with flour. Brown rolls in hot shortening. Cook, covered, over low heat 15 to 20 minutes, turning occasionally.

Remove rolls; reserve pan juices. Serve with *Gravy:* In skillet blend 2 tablespoons reserved pan juices with 2 tablespoons all-purpose flour. Dissolve 1 beef bouillon cube in 1 cup boiling water; add to flour mixture with ⅓ cup light cream. Cook and stir till bubbly. Add ¼ teaspoon salt. Heat through. Serves 4.

BEEF BALL OVEN STEW

Combine 1 beaten egg; ½ cup milk; ¼ cup yellow cornmeal; 2 tablespoons chopped green pepper; 1 tablespoon instant minced onion; 1 teaspoon dry mustard; ¾ teaspoon salt; and ½ to 1 teaspoon chili powder. Add 1 pound ground beef; mix. Form 12 balls.

Lightly coat meatballs in 2 tablespoons all-purpose flour, reserving remaining flour. Brown in 2 tablespoons hot shortening. Place meatballs in 3-quart casserole, reserving pan juices. To casserole, add 3 potatoes, peeled and quartered; 3 medium onions, quartered; and 6 carrots, peeled and cut in thin strips 2 inches long. Season with salt and pepper.

Blend reserved flour (about 4 teaspoons) into reserved pan juices in skillet. Stir in one 18-ounce can tomato juice and ½ bay leaf, crushed. Cook and stir till thickened and bubbly. Pour atop casserole. Cover; bake at 350° for 1 to 1¼ hours. Serves 6.

CHEESY STUFFED BURGERS

1 3-ounce can chopped mushrooms
2 tablespoons chopped onion
2 tablespoons butter or margarine
1 cup dry bread cubes (about 2
    slices cut in ½-inch cubes)
1 pound ground beef
1 6-ounce can (⅔ cup) evaporated
    milk
1 10¾-ounce can condensed
    Cheddar cheese soup

Drain mushrooms, reserving liquid. Cook onion in butter. Combine onion with ¼ *cup* of the mushrooms, bread cubes, ¼ teaspoon salt, and dash pepper; toss with 2 to 3 tablespoons mushroom liquid or till moist.

Mix ground beef with ⅓ *cup* of the evaporated milk and ½ teaspoon salt. On waxed paper shape meat into 5 circles, each 6-inches in diameter. Spoon about ¼ cup stuffing in center of each circle. Pull up edges over stuffing and seal. Bake in 1½-quart casserole, uncovered, at 350° for 45 minutes.

Combine cheese soup with remaining mushrooms and remaining evaporated milk; heat through. To serve, spoon sauce over burgers. Garnish with parsley, if desired. Serves 5.

STUFFED MEAT ROLLS

Combine 1 pound ground beef, ¼ cup milk, ¾ teaspoon salt, and dash pepper; mix well. Pat mixture into four 4-inch squares. Cook ¼ cup chopped celery and ¼ cup chopped onion in 2 tablespoons butter or margarine till tender but not brown. Add 1 cup soft bread crumbs; mix well. Season.

Divide stuffing among meat squares. Roll up; seal ends. Brown in 2 tablespoons hot shortening. Place in 10x6x1½-inch baking dish. Dissolve 1 beef bouillon cube in 1 cup boiling water; pour over meat rolls. Cover and bake at 350° for 40 to 45 minutes, turning once. Remove rolls, reserving meat juices.

Blend 3 tablespoons all-purpose flour with ¼ cup milk. Stir into reserved meat juices in skillet; add ½ teaspoon dried basil leaves, crushed. Cook, stirring constantly, till thickened and bubbly. Cook 2 minutes longer. Serve with meat rolls. Makes 4 servings.

King-sized meatballs stuffed and sauced with canned cheese soup are certain to please the family. These Cheesy Stuffed Burgers feature ground beef in a recipe reminiscent of the popular sandwich.

Experiment with the different flavored canned soups when preparing the hurry-up sauce. Another time, used packaged herb-seasoned stuffing mix. Just follow package directions to create a jiffy entree.

PORCUPINE MEATBALLS

1 beaten egg
1 10¾-ounce can condensed
   tomato soup
¼ cup uncooked long-grain rice
2 tablespoons finely chopped onion
1 tablespoon snipped parsley
½ teaspoon salt
   Dash pepper
1 pound ground beef
1 teaspoon Worcestershire sauce

Combine egg, ¼ *cup* of the tomato soup, and next 5 ingredients. Add beef; mix well. Shape into 20 meatballs; place in skillet. Mix remaining soup, ½ cup water, and Worcestershire sauce. Pour over meatballs. Bring to boiling; reduce heat. Simmer, covered, for 40 minutes, stirring often. Makes 4 or 5 servings.

ZWIEBACK MEATBALLS

·Combine 1 beaten egg, ⅓ cup milk, ½ cup crushed zwieback (4 to 5 slices), 1 tablespoon finely chopped onion, ½ teaspoon salt, ¼ teaspoon ground nutmeg, and dash pepper. Add 1 pound ground beef; mix well. Shape into 20 balls. Brown in 1 tablespoon hot shortening. Remove from skillet; discard drippings.

Dissolve 1 beef bouillon cube in ¾ cup boiling water. Blend 2 tablespoons all-purpose flour with ¼ cup cold water. In skillet stir flour mixture into bouillon. Cook and stir till thick and bubbly. Return balls to skillet. Cover; simmer 20 minutes. Serves 4 or 5.

GOURMET MEATBALLS

Combine 1 beaten egg, ⅓ cup milk, ½ cup soft bread crumbs, ¼ cup chopped onion, ¼ teaspoon salt, and dash pepper. Add 1 pound ground beef and ¼ pound braunschweiger; mix well. Shape into 18 balls. Chill 1 hour.

In skillet brown balls in 2 tablespoons hot shortening; shake pan often to keep balls round. Drain off fat. Blend one 10½-ounce can condensed cream of mushroom soup with ⅓ cup milk; pour over balls. Cover; bring to boiling. Reduce heat; simmer 15 to 20 minutes. Serve over noodles. Serves 5 or 6.

CHERRY-SAUCED HAM BALLS

As pictured opposite chapter introduction—

1 beaten egg
3 tablespoons milk
⅓ cup fine dry bread crumbs
1½ pounds ground fully-cooked ham
2 tablespoons shortening
1 21-ounce can cherry pie filling
1 tablespoon lemon juice
½ teaspoon ground cinnamon
   Dash ground cloves

Combine first 3 ingredients and dash pepper. Add ham; mix well. Shape into 18 balls. Brown balls in hot shortening, shaking pan often to keep balls round. Drain off fat. Add ¼ cup water. Simmer, covered, 15 to 20 minutes, turning balls occasionally. Meanwhile, heat pie filling with remaining ingredients and 2 tablespoons water. Serve some sauce atop balls; pass remainder. Serves 6.

SPANISH-STYLE MEATBALLS

1 beaten egg
⅛ cup milk
1 cup soft bread crumbs
1½ pounds ground beef
4 slices bacon
½ cup chopped celery
¼ cup chopped green pepper
¼ cup finely chopped onion
1 16-ounce can tomatoes, cut up
1 bay leaf
2 teaspoons cornstarch

Combine egg, milk, crumbs, 1 teaspoon salt, and dash pepper. Add beef; mix well. Shape into 12 meatballs. Cook bacon till crisp; drain, reserving drippings. Crumble bacon; set aside. In 2 tablespoons reserved drippings, cook celery, green pepper, and onion till tender; set aside. Brown meatballs in remaining reserved drippings. Drain off fat.

Add bacon, vegetable mixture, tomatoes, and bay leaf to balls. Cover; cook 20 to 25 minutes. Discard bay leaf; remove balls. Blend cornstarch with 2 tablespoons cold water; stir into tomato mixture. Cook and stir till bubbly. Serve over balls. Serves 6.

LAMB BALLS IN CHILI

Tender meatballs simmer in a spicy chili sauce before being served over fluffy hot rice—

⅓ cup milk
1 cup soft bread crumbs
    (about 1½ slices)
1 pound ground lamb
2 tablespoons shortening
1 16-ounce can tomatoes, cut up
1 16-ounce can red kidney beans,
    drained
½ cup chopped onion
¼ cup chopped green pepper
1 teaspoon chili powder
    Hot cooked rice

Combine milk, bread crumbs, and ½ teaspoon salt. Add lamb and mix thoroughly. Shape mixture into 24 meatballs. Brown meatballs in hot shortening in skillet. Drain off excess fat. Add tomatoes, kidney beans, onion, green pepper, chili powder, and ¼ teaspoon salt. Cover and cook over low heat for 20 minutes, stirring occasionally. Uncover and cook 5 to 10 minutes, or till sauce is desired consistency. Serve meatballs over hot cooked rice. Makes 4 to 6 servings.

LAMB-EGGPLANT BALLS

Dry mustard sparks meatballs in tomato sauce—

1 beaten egg
⅓ cup soft bread crumbs (½ slice)
2 cups chopped, peeled eggplant
½ cup chopped onion
1 teaspoon snipped parsley
1 teaspoon salt
⅛ teaspoon pepper
1½ pounds ground lamb
3 tablespoons salad oil
1 8-ounce can tomato sauce
⅛ teaspoon dry mustard

Combine first 7 ingredients; add lamb and mix well. Shape into 18 meatballs. In skillet brown meatballs in hot oil. Drain off fat. Blend tomato sauce with mustard; pour over balls. Simmer, covered, for 30 minutes. Uncover; cook 15 minutes more. Serves 6.

MEAT AND POTATO BALLS

1 beaten egg
2 tablespoons milk
¼ cup fine dry bread crumbs
1 cup finely shredded, peeled, raw
    potato, drained (1 large)
¼ cup chopped green onion with
    tops
1 teaspoon prepared mustard
¾ teaspoon salt
⅛ teaspoon pepper
1 pound ground pork
2 tablespoons shortening
1 chicken bouillon cube
2 tablespoons all-purpose flour

Combine first 8 ingredients. Add pork; mix well. Shape into 24 meatballs. In skillet brown meatballs in hot shortening; drain off fat. Dissolve bouillon cube in 1 cup boiling water; add to meatballs in skillet. Cover and cook over low heat for 20 minutes, turning occasionally. Remove meatballs to serving bowl; reserve pan drippings. Blend flour with ⅓ cup cold water; stir into reserved drippings. Cook and stir till thick and bubbly. Serve with meatballs. Makes 4 to 6 servings.

Lamb-Eggplant Balls combine the meat and vegetable in one dish. Accompany with hot buttered noodles and salad.

Meal-in-a-dish Favorites

SPANISH NOODLES

In large skillet cook 2 slices bacon till crisp; drain, reserving drippings. Crumble bacon; set aside. Add ½ cup chopped onion to reserved drippings in skillet; cook till tender. Add 1 pound ground beef; brown.

Stir in one 28-ounce can tomatoes, cut up; ½ cup chopped green pepper; ¼ cup chili sauce; 1 teaspoon salt; and dash pepper. Stir in 4 ounces uncooked medium noodles. Cook, covered, over low heat for 30 minutes or till noodles are tender, stirring frequently. Stir in bacon. Makes 4 servings.

HAM SQUARES

    1 beaten egg
    ¾ cup milk
    1 cup soft bread crumbs (about
        1½ slices)
    2 tablespoons chopped onion
    2 teaspoons snipped parsley
    1 teaspoon dry mustard
    ½ teaspoon salt
      Dash pepper
    1 pound ground fully-cooked ham
    ½ pound ground beef
      Curried Cream Peas

Combine egg, milk, crumbs, onion, parsley, dry mustard, salt, and pepper. Add ham and beef; mix well. Lightly pack meat mixture into 10x6x1½-inch baking dish. Bake, uncovered, at 325° for 1 hour. Spoon off drippings. Allow the meat to stand a few minutes before cutting into squares.

Top squares with *Curried Creamed Peas:* Cook one 10-ounce package frozen peas according to package directions; drain thoroughly. Melt 2 tablespoons butter or margarine in saucepan. Blend in 1 tablespoon all-purpose flour, ¼ teaspoon curry powder, ¼ teaspoon salt, and dash white pepper. Add 1 cup milk; cook and stir till mixture thickens and bubbles. Cook 1 minute more. Stir in the cooked peas. Makes 6 servings.

BEEF-SAUSAGE BALLS

    1 beaten egg
    1 cup milk
    ¾ cup finely crushed saltine
        cracker crumbs (21 crackers)
    ¼ cup finely chopped celery
    1 tablespoon snipped parsley
    ½ teaspoon salt
    ¼ teaspoon ground sage
      Dash pepper
    1 pound ground beef
    ½ pound bulk pork sausage
      Parmesan Grits Ring
      Tomato-Onion Sauce

Combine egg, milk, crumbs, celery, parsley, and seasonings. Add beef and sausage; mix well. Shape into 1-inch balls. Place in shallow baking pan. Bake at 375° for 25 to 30 minutes. Drain. Place meatballs in center of Parmesan Grits Ring and drizzle with Tomato-Onion Sauce. Pass extra sauce. Serves 8.

Parmesan Grits Ring: Combine 5 cups water and 1½ teaspoons salt; bring to boiling. Slowly stir in 1¼ cups quick-cooking hominy grits. Cook, covered, over low heat for 25 to 30 minutes, stirring occasionally. Remove from heat. Pour into 5-cup ring mold which has been rinsed with cold water. Let stand 25 minutes. Unmold ring onto large oven-proof platter. Combine 1 beaten egg and 1 tablespoon salad oil; brush on grits ring. Combine ¼ cup fine dry bread crumbs and ¼ cup grated Parmesan cheese. Sprinkle over ring. Bake at 375° for 8 to 10 minutes, or till grits ring is golden brown.

Tomato-Onion Sauce: In saucepan cook ¼ cup sliced green onion with tops in 1 tablespoon butter till tender but not brown. Blend in one 10¾-ounce can condensed tomato soup, 2 tablespoons water, 1 teaspoon Worcestershire sauce, and dash pepper. Heat.

Three dishes that soon will be family favorites are Spanish Noodles, Ham → Squares, and Beef-Sausage Balls.

LAMB ROLL-UPS

So good with a foamy, fluffy lemon sauce—

12 large romaine leaves
 1 slightly beaten egg yolk
 ½ cup milk
 ⅓ cup uncooked packaged
       precooked rice
 ½ cup chopped onion
 ¾ teaspoon salt
    Dash pepper
 1 pound ground lamb
 ½ cup canned condensed beef broth

· · ·

 1 egg
 1 egg white
1½ tablespoons lemon juice

Soften romaine leaves by dipping leaves in very hot water, then crushing the rib with thumb. Mix together the egg yolk, milk, uncooked rice, onion, salt, and pepper. Add lamb and mix thoroughly. Shape mixture into twelve 3-inch long rolls, using about ¼ cup meat mixture for each. Place each roll lengthwise on a softened romaine leaf. Fold sides up over meat so they overlap and tuck in ends; secure with wooden picks. Place rolls in a skillet and pour broth over. Cover; simmer 30 minutes. Pour off broth and strain; reserve for Lemon Sauce.

For Lemon Sauce, beat whole egg with egg white till thick. Slowly beat in lemon juice and reserved cooking broth. In saucepan stir over low heat till mixture thickens slightly.

Place lamb roll-ups on warm serving platter. Remove wooden picks. Spoon some sauce over rolls and pass remainder. Serves 4 to 6.

A tasty tomato sauce that smothers Stuffed Cabbage Rolls is the perfect complement to a beef and rice mixture.

Cabbage rolls are easy to make when the leaf is limp. Place meat mixture on leaf, carefully tuck in sides, then roll up.

STUFFED CABBAGE ROLLS

12 large cabbage leaves
 1 beaten egg
 ¼ cup water
 1 cup cooked long-grain rice
 ¼ cup chopped onion
1¼ teaspoons salt
 ¼ teaspoon pepper
 ¼ teaspoon dried thyme leaves,
       crushed
1¼ pounds ground beef
 1 8-ounce can tomato sauce
 1 tablespoon brown sugar
 1 tablespoon lemon juice

Immerse cabbage leaves (heavy center vein of leaf may be cut out about 2 inches) in boiling water for 3 minutes or just till limp; drain. Combine next 7 ingredients. Add beef; mix thoroughly. Place about ¼ cup meat mixture in center of each leaf; fold in sides and roll ends over meat. Fasten with wooden picks; place in large skillet.

Combine remaining ingredients. Pour over cabbage rolls. Simmer, covered, 1 hour, basting occasionally. Remove cover for last 5 minutes or till sauce is of desired consistency. Makes 6 servings.

BEEF-FILLED SQUASH

  2 medium-large acorn squash
  4 slices bacon, diced
  1 pound ground beef
  ¼ cup chopped onion
  1 to 2 tablespoons milk
  ¼ cup crushed potato chips

Cut squash in half lengthwise; remove seeds. Bake cut side down in shallow pan at 350° for 45 minutes or till tender. Fry diced bacon. Add beef, onion, ½ teaspoon salt, and dash pepper; cook till beef is browned. Pour off excess fat. Remove squash from shells (reserve shells). In small mixing bowl whip squash with ½ teaspoon salt; add milk as needed to make mixture fluffy. Combine with beef mixture. Return to squash shells. Top with crushed potato chips. Continue baking at 350° for 15 minutes. Makes 4 servings.

Potato chips are the crunchy topper for Beef-Filled Squash. Trim the plate with bright red spiced crab apples.

SAUCY CABBAGE ROLLS

  6 large cabbage leaves
  1 beaten egg
  ½ cup milk
  ¾ cup cooked long-grain rice
  ½ teaspoon salt
  ¼ teaspoon dried dillweed
  ⅛ teaspoon pepper
  1 pound ground beef

     • • •

  1 10½-ounce can mushroom gravy
  ¼ cup catsup
  ⅛ cup water
  ⅛ cup finely chopped onion
  ¼ teaspoon dried dillweed

Immerse cabbage leaves (heavy center vein of leaf may be cut out about 2 inches) in boiling water for 3 minutes or just till limp; drain. Combine egg, milk, rice, salt, ¼ teaspoon dillweed, and pepper. Add beef; mix well. Place about ½ cup meat mixture in center of each cabbage leaf; fold in sides and roll ends over meat.

In skillet combine remaining ingredients. Add cabbage rolls. Cover and cook over low heat 30 minutes, stirring occasionally. Uncover and cook 15 minutes longer, stirring occasionally. Makes 6 servings.

SAUSAGE-STUFFED SQUASH

Meat and vegetable all in one—

  3 medium acorn squash
  1 pound bulk pork sausage
  ¼ cup chopped green pepper
  ¼ cup chopped onion
  1 1½-ounce envelope cheese
     sauce mix
  1 3-ounce can chopped mushrooms,
     drained (½ cup)
  ½ cup fine dry bread crumbs
  1 tablespoon butter or margarine,
     melted

Cut squash in half lengthwise; remove seeds. Bake cut side down in shallow pan at 350° for 35 to 40 minutes or till tender.

Meanwhile, in skillet cook sausage with green pepper and onion till meat is brown and vegetables are crisp-tender; drain off excess fat. Blend cheese sauce mix with meat; add liquid following package directions. Cook, stirring constantly, till thickened and bubbly. Stir in drained mushrooms.

Fill squash cavities with sausage mixture. Combine bread crumbs with melted butter. Sprinkle atop squash. Continue baking for 15 to 20 minutes or till crumbs are lightly browned. Makes 6 servings.

VEGETABLE-MEAT CUPS

As pictured opposite contents page—

1 beaten egg
¼ cup milk
¼ cup coarsely crushed saltine
   cracker crumbs (6 crackers)
¾ teaspoon salt
½ teaspoon Worcestershire sauce
1 pound ground beef
   Packaged instant mashed potatoes
   (enough for 4 servings)
2 tablespoons sliced green onion
½ 10¾-ounce can condensed cheddar
   cheese soup (⅔ cup)
3 tablespoons milk
½ 10-ounce package frozen peas,
   cooked and drained

Combine first 5 ingredients and dash pepper. Add beef; mix well. On 4 squares waxed paper shape into 4 patties with 5-inch diameter. Shape each over an inverted 5-ounce custard cup; discard paper. Chill 1 hour.

Place inverted cups in shallow baking pan; bake at 375° for 20 minutes. Prepare potatoes following package directions; stir in onion. Lift baked meat cups from custard cups and turn upright; fill with potatoes. In saucepan mix soup with 3 tablespoons milk; stir in peas. Heat. Spoon over meat cups. Garnish with parsley, if desired. Serves 4.

SAUSAGE-STUFFED APPLES

½ pound bulk pork sausage
¼ cup chopped onion
4 large baking apples
¼ cup finely crushed saltine
   cracker crumbs (7 crackers)
1 beaten egg

Break up sausage in skillet; cook slowly with onion till meat is browned. Drain off fat. Core apples. Scoop out pulp leaving shells ½ inch thick; reserve pulp. Peel shells one quarter way down. Chop reserved pulp (about 1¼ cups); add to meat with crumbs, egg, ¼ teaspoon salt, and dash pepper. Mix well. Stuff apples with meat mixture. Bake at 375° for 40 minutes or till tender. Serves 4.

STUFFED PEPPER CUPS

As pictured on front cover—

6 medium green peppers
1 pound ground beef
⅓ cup chopped onion
1 16-ounce can tomatoes, cut up
½ cup uncooked long-grain rice
1 teaspoon Worcestershire sauce
4 ounces sharp process American
   cheese, shredded (1 cup)

Cut off tops of green peppers; remove seeds and membrane. Scallop edges. Precook peppers in boiling salted water 5 minutes; drain. (For crisp peppers, omit precooking.) Sprinkle inside of cups generously with salt.

Brown meat with onion. Add ½ teaspoon salt and dash pepper. Stir in tomatoes, rice, ½ cup water, and Worcestershire. Cover; simmer 15 minutes. Stir in cheese. Stuff peppers; place in 10x6x1½-inch baking dish. Bake at 350° for 20 to 25 minutes. Serves 6.

STUFFED TOMATO CUPS

4 large tomatoes
   Dried basil leaves, crushed
½ pound ground beef
¼ cup chopped onion
⅔ cup herb-seasoned stuffing
   croutons
¼ teaspoon Worcestershire sauce
4 teaspoons grated Parmesan cheese

Cut tops off tomatoes; scoop out pulp. Chop tops and pulp; drain. Cut sawtooth edges around shells; drain. Sprinkle inside with salt and basil. In skillet brown beef with onion; drain. Stir in pulp, croutons, ½ teaspoon salt, and Worcestershire; stuff shells.

Sprinkle tomatoes with cheese. Place in shallow baking dish; fill dish with ½-inch water. Bake at 375° for 25 to 30 minutes. Trim with parsley, if desired. Serves 4.

Plump tomato shells blossom when filled→ with herb-seasoned ground beef. These Stuffed Tomato Cups are garnished with parsley and grated Parmesan cheese.

MEATBALL-KRAUT SKILLET

  1 beaten egg
¼ cup milk
  3 cups soft bread crumbs
    (about 4 slices)
¾ teaspoon salt
    Dash pepper
  1 pound ground beef
  2 tablespoons shortening
  1 27-ounce can sauerkraut, drained
½ cup chopped onion
¾ cup uncooked long-grain rice
  1 16-ounce can tomatoes, cut up

Combine first 5 ingredients. Add beef; mix well. Shape into 12 meatballs. Brown in hot shortening in large skillet. Remove balls; pour off fat. In same skillet combine sauerkraut, onion, and ½ teaspoon salt. Stir in rice and 1½ cups water. Add balls and tomatoes. Bring to boiling; reduce heat and simmer, covered, for 30 to 35 minutes. Serves 6.

For easy Meatball-Kraut Skillet add meatballs to a sauerkraut and rice mixture. Tomatoes give color and flavor.

VEAL CHILI

Serve over corn bread made from a mix—

Cook 1 pound ground veal; ¼ cup chopped onion; and 1 small clove garlic, crushed, in saucepan till meat is lightly browned and onion is tender. Stir in one 16-ounce can tomatoes, cut up; 2 teaspoons brown sugar; 2 teaspoons wine vinegar; 1 bay leaf; ½ teaspoon salt; ½ teaspoon dried oregano leaves, crushed; and ½ teaspoon chili powder. Bring to boiling. Cover and simmer 1 hour, stirring occasionally. Discard bay leaf.

Stir in ¼ cup sliced pimiento-stuffed green olives and simmer, uncovered, 30 minutes longer. Mix 2 teaspoons cornstarch and 1 tablespoon cold water. Stir into chili mixture. Cook and stir till mixture thickens and bubbles. Spoon chili over squares of corn bread. Makes 6 servings.

BEEF AND PORK STEW

  1 pound ground beef
  1 pound ground pork
½ cup chopped onion
  1 17-ounce can whole kernel
    corn, undrained
  1 16-ounce can tomatoes, cut up
  1 chicken bouillon cube
⅛ cup catsup
  1 tablespoon sugar
  1 tablespoon lemon juice
½ teaspoon salt
¼ teaspoon dried rosemary leaves,
    crushed
  1 bay leaf
  4 drops bottled hot pepper sauce
    Dash freshly ground pepper
¾ cup soft bread crumbs
    (about 1 slice)

In large skillet brown meats and cook onion until tender; drain off excess fat. Add corn, tomatoes, and bouillon cube dissolved in 1 cup boiling water. Blend catsup, sugar, lemon juice, salt, rosemary, bay leaf, hot pepper sauce, and pepper; stir into stew. Add bread crumbs. Bring to boiling; reduce heat. Simmer, covered, about 45 to 60 minutes. Remove bay leaf before serving. Serves 6 to 8.

Fluffy rice is a must with Beef Oriental. For attractive servings, lightly press hot cooked rice into custard cups and unmold in dishes. Trim with parsley.

CHILI RICE

Here's Spanish rice with ground meat added—

> 1 pound ground beef
> ½ cup chopped celery
> ¼ cup chopped onion
> ¼ cup chopped green pepper
> 1 clove garlic, minced
> 2 teaspoons salt
> 3 cups water
> 1 16-ounce can tomatoes, cut up
> 1 cup uncooked long-grain rice
> 1 6-ounce can tomato paste
> 1 teaspoon sugar
> 1 teaspoon chili powder
> 1 bay leaf

Brown beef in large saucepan; drain off excess fat. Add next 5 ingredients; cook till vegetables are crisp-tender. Stir in remaining ingredients. Cover and simmer 25 minutes or till rice is done; stir occasionally. Remove bay leaf. Makes 8 servings.

BEEF ORIENTAL

Cauliflowerets add crispness—

Pour boiling water over one 7-ounce package frozen Chinese pea pods and carefully break apart with fork; drain immediately.

In skillet cook 1 pound lean ground beef in 1 tablespoon salad oil till brown. Push beef to one side of skillet. Add ¼ cup chopped onion and 1 small clove garlic, minced; cook just a few seconds. Add 4 cups (1 medium head) thinly sliced raw cauliflowerets and 1 cup canned condensed beef broth. Cook 3 minutes or till cauliflower is crisp-tender, stirring gently during cooking.

Mix together 2 tablespoons cornstarch, ½ teaspoon monosodium glutamate, ½ cup cold water, and ¼ cup soy sauce till blended. Stir into mixture in skillet. Add the pea pods. Cook, stirring constantly, till sauce thickens and bubbles. Serve with fluffy hot cooked rice. Pass additional soy sauce, if desired. Makes 6 servings.

STACK-A-DINNER

    1 pound ground beef
    ½ cup chopped onion
    1 8-ounce can tomato sauce with
        mushrooms
    ¼ cup catsup
    ½ teaspoon dried oregano leaves,
        crushed
    3 drops bottled hot pepper sauce
    2 cups uncooked packaged
        precooked rice
    1 10-ounce package frozen peas
    4 ounces sharp process American
        cheese, shredded (1 cup)
      Sliced pimiento-stuffed green
        olives

In skillet brown meat with onion; drain off fat. Add tomato sauce, next 3 ingredients, ¼ cup water, ¼ teaspoon salt, and dash pepper; bring to boiling, stirring often. Cook rice and prepare peas following package directions. On individual serving plates, layer rice, peas, meat mixture, then cheese. Trim with olives. Makes 6 servings.

BEEF AND OKRA SKILLET

    2 pounds ground beef
    1 15-ounce can tomato sauce
    1 12-ounce can whole kernel corn,
        undrained
    1 10-ounce package frozen okra,
        thawed and cut into ¾-inch
        pieces
    1 tablespoon brown sugar
    4 slices sharp process American
        cheese

In skillet brown meat; drain. Sprinkle with ½ teaspoon salt. Add tomato sauce, undrained corn, okra, and brown sugar. Bring to boiling; reduce heat. Cover; simmer 10 minutes. Arrange cheese slices atop. Cover; heat 3 to 4 minutes to melt cheese. Serves 8.

←Stack-a-Dinner features a complete meal-in-one. Vary the vegetable and garnish to accommodate family tastes, then serve over hot rice, spaghetti, or noodles.

HAM SPAGHETTI

    In saucepan cook 2 cups coarsely ground fully-cooked ham; ½ cup chopped onion; and ¼ cup chopped green pepper in 2 tablespoons hot shortening till meat is lightly browned. Stir in one 16-ounce can tomatoes, cut up. Simmer, uncovered, 25 to 30 minutes. Stir in 2 ounces sharp process American cheese, shredded (½ cup); heat till melted. Serve ham sauce over hot cooked spaghetti, macaroni, *or* rice. Makes 8 servings.

MACARONI-BEEF SUPPER

  1½ pounds ground beef
    1 cup chopped onion
    1 clove garlic, minced
    2 8-ounce cans tomato sauce
    1 6-ounce can (1⅛ cups) sliced
        mushrooms, undrained
    1 7-ounce package macaroni,
        cooked and drained
    1 tablespoon vinegar
    1 teaspoon salt
    1 teaspoon chili powder
    1 teaspoon Worcestershire sauce
    5 ounces process American cheese,
        shredded (1¼ cups)

In skillet cook beef, onion, and garlic till onion is tender, leaving beef in bite-size pieces; drain off fat. Stir in ½ cup water and remaining ingredients, except cheese. Cover; cook slowly 25 minutes. Stir in *1 cup* of the cheese. Turn into serving dish. Garnish with remaining cheese. Makes 6 servings.

RUSSIAN SKILLET SUPPER

    In skillet cook 1 pound bulk pork sausage, ½ cup chopped onion, and ¼ cup chopped green pepper till meat is browned, breaking up sausage as it cooks; drain off fat. Add one 16-ounce can tomatoes with liquid, cut up; 1 cup uncooked elbow macaroni; ½ cup tomato juice *or* water; 1 tablespoon sugar; 1 teaspoon salt; and ½ teaspoon chili powder. Cover; simmer 20 minutes, stirring frequently. Stir in 1 cup dairy sour cream; heat through, *but do not boil*. Makes 4 or 5 servings.

MEXICAN-STYLE HASH

    2 cups coarsely ground or diced
        cooked roast beef
    ⅓ cup chopped onion
    2 tablespoons shortening
    1½ cups finely chopped raw potatoes
    1 12-ounce can whole kernel corn,
        drained
    1 10¾-ounce can condensed
        tomato soup
    ¼ teaspoon chili powder

Cook beef and onion in shortening in oven-going skillet till onion is tender. Add potatoes, corn, tomato soup, and chili powder; stir to mix. Cover with foil. Bake at 350° for 35 to 40 minutes. Makes 4 servings.

SKILLET HASH

In skillet cook ⅓ cup finely chopped onion in 2 tablespoons butter or margarine till tender but not brown. Add 2 cups ground or diced cooked roast beef; 2 or 3 medium raw potatoes, diced or ground; ½ cup beef broth or leftover gravy; and ½ teaspoon salt. Mix well. Cover; cook over low heat, stirring often till potatoes are tender, about 15 minutes. Makes 4 servings.

ENGLISH HASH

A variation of the English Bubble and Squeak—

    4 cups chopped cabbage
    ½ cup finely chopped onion
    ¼ cup salad oil
    2 cups finely chopped cooked
        potatoes
    1 to 1½ cups ground cooked
        roast beef
    ½ cup gravy (canned or leftover)

Cook cabbage in boiling salted water; drain. In 10-inch skillet cook onion in salad oil until tender. Mix drained cabbage, potatoes, meat, gravy, 1 teaspoon salt, and dash pepper; toss with onion. Pat solidly into same skillet. Heat through until crust forms. Invert on platter. Cut in wedges. Serves 4 to 6.

TANGIERS HASH

In skillet slowly cook ½ cup chopped onion with 1 pound bulk pork sausage till sausage is browned, breaking up sausage as it cooks; drain. Stir in 2 cups ground cooked roast beef and 3 medium tomatoes, peeled and chopped (1½ cups). Divide evenly among 4 or 5 individual casseroles.

Top with ¼ cup snipped parsley. Combine ½ cup fine dry bread crumbs and 2 tablespoons butter or margarine, melted. Sprinkle over parsley. Bake, uncovered, at 350° for 30 to 35 minutes or till hot. Makes 4 or 5 servings.

BEEF AND DUMPLINGS

    1 beaten egg
    1 10½-ounce can condensed cream
        of celery soup
    ½ cup soft bread crumbs
    2 tablespoons dry onion soup mix
    1 pound ground beef
    2 tablespoons shortening
    1 tablespoon all-purpose flour
    ½ teaspoon paprika
    ½ cup water
    1 3-ounce can (⅔ cup) chopped
        mushrooms, undrained
    Dumplings

Combine egg, ¼ *cup* of the soup, crumbs, and dry soup mix. Add beef; mix well. Shape into 8 meatballs. In skillet brown meatballs in hot shortening. Drain off excess fat. Blend together remaining soup, flour, and paprika. Gradually stir in water. Add mushrooms with liquid. Pour over meatballs in skillet. Bring to boiling; reduce heat and simmer, covered, for 20 minutes. Pour into 1½-quart casserole. Top with Dumplings. Bake, uncovered, at 400° for 20 to 25 minutes. Makes 4 servings.

Dumplings: Combine 1 cup sifted all-purpose flour, 2 teaspoons baking powder, 1 teaspoon dry onion soup mix, and ¼ teaspoon celery salt. Combine ½ cup milk and 1 tablespoon salad oil. Stir into flour mixture till smooth. Combine 1 cup soft bread crumbs with 2 tablespoons melted butter. Divide dough into 8 portions; drop by tablespoon into buttered crumbs, turning to coat all sides. Place dumplings atop *boiling* meat mixture.

GROUND BEEF YORKSHIRE

A takeoff on classic Yorkshire pudding—

  1 cup sifted all-purpose flour
  1 teaspoon baking powder
  1 teaspoon salt
  3 well-beaten eggs
1½ cups milk
  ¼ cup butter or margarine, melted
  2 tablespoons snipped parsley
  1 pound ground round
  ¼ cup finely chopped onion
  ¼ cup diced celery
    Dash pepper
    Shortening
    Speedy Mushroom Sauce

Sift flour, baking powder, and salt together. Combine eggs, milk, and butter. Add to flour mixture; beat till well blended. Stir in parsley. Combine meat, onion, celery, and pepper; mix thoroughly. Shape into 16 logs 2½ inches long; brown in hot shortening.

Place logs in greased 8x8x2-inch baking dish. Pour batter over logs. Bake at 350° for 45 minutes. Serve with *Speedy Mushroom Sauce:* Combine one 10½-ounce can condensed cream of mushroom soup and ⅓ cup milk. Heat thoroughly. Serves 6 to 8.

HAM STRATA

  3 tablespoons butter, softened
  1 tablespoon prepared mustard
  6 slices white bread
1½ cups ground fully-cooked ham
  4 beaten eggs
  2 cups milk
  ¼ teaspoon salt
    Dash pepper

Combine butter and mustard. Spread on one side of each bread slice. Cut each slice in thirds. Arrange *half* the bread, buttered side up, in greased 8x8x2-inch baking dish. Sprinkle ham evenly over top. Cover with remaining bread, buttered side down.

Mix eggs, milk, and seasonings; pour over all. Bake at 325° about 50 minutes or till set. Let stand a few minutes before serving. Cut into squares. Makes 6 servings.

HAM AND NOODLES

Cook 4 ounces noodles in boiling salted water according to package directions; drain. Cook ¼ cup chopped green pepper in 2 tablespoons butter till tender. In bowl combine 1 beaten egg; ¼ cup milk; one 17-ounce can cream-style corn; and 3 ounces sharp process American cheese, shredded (¾ cup).

Mix in 1 pound coarsely ground fully-cooked ham (3 cups), green pepper, and noodles. Turn into 2-quart casserole. Combine ½ cup cornflakes, crushed, and 1 tablespoon melted butter. Sprinkle atop. Bake at 350° for 50 to 60 minutes. Serves 6.

CARROT-APPLE-HAM BAKE

  4 large carrots, peeled and
    sliced crosswise (2 cups)
  4 cooking apples, peeled and
    thickly sliced (4 cups)
  ¼ cup brown sugar
  1 tablespoon butter or margarine
  1 beaten egg
  ¼ cup milk
  ½ cup soft bread crumbs
  2 cups ground fully-cooked ham
    Shortening

Simmer carrots in salted water for 10 minutes; drain. In 2-quart casserole layer carrots, then apples, and brown sugar. Dot with butter. Combine egg, milk, and crumbs. Add ham and mix well. Shape into 8 patties. Brown in hot shortening. Lay patties atop apples. Bake, covered, at 350° for 45 minutes. Serves 4.

HAM AND MUSHROOM BAKE

In large bowl gradually blend ½ cup milk into one 10¾-ounce can condensed Cheddar cheese soup. Stir in one 3-ounce can sliced mushrooms, drained; ½ cup chopped celery; and 2 cups ground or finely chopped fully-cooked ham. Cook 3 ounces medium noodles in *unsalted* water. Drain; add to soup mixture. Turn into 10x6x1½-inch baking dish. Mix ⅔ cup soft bread crumbs with 1 tablespoon melted butter; sprinkle atop casserole. Bake at 375° about 30 minutes. Serves 4 or 5.

SAUSAGE-NOODLE BAKE

- 1 pound bulk pork sausage
- 4 ounces corkscrew macaroni
- 1 10½-ounce can condensed cream of chicken soup
- ½ cup milk
- 2 tablespoons *each* chopped green pepper and chopped canned pimiento
- 1 cup soft bread crumbs
- 1 tablespoon butter, melted

In skillet brown sausage, breaking up sausage as it cooks; drain. Cook noodles in boiling *unsalted* water till tender; drain. Blend together soup and milk. Stir in noodles, green pepper, pimiento, and sausage. Turn into 1½-quart casserole. Combine crumbs and butter; sprinkle atop. Bake, uncovered, at 350° for 40 minutes. Makes 5 or 6 servings.

SAUSAGE-POTATO SCALLOP

In skillet brown 1 pound bulk pork sausage, breaking up sausage as it cooks. Drain off fat. Peel and thinly slice 4 medium potatoes (4 cups). Place *half* the potatoes in 2-quart casserole. Sift 2 tablespoons all-purpose flour and ⅛ teaspoon salt over potatoes.

Top with *half* the sausage and ½ cup shredded sharp process American cheese. Repeat with remaining potatoes, 2 tablespoons flour, ⅛ teaspoon salt, remaining sausage, and ½ cup shredded cheese. Pour 1½ cups milk over all. Cover; bake at 350° for 50 to 60 minutes or till potatoes are tender. Uncover; bake 10 minutes more. Makes 4 to 6 servings.

CHILI HOMINY BAKE

In skillet brown 1½ pounds ground beef and ½ cup chopped onion. Drain off excess fat. Sprinkle with 2 tablespoons all-purpose flour and 1 teaspoon salt. Add one 20-ounce can hominy, drained; one 16-ounce can tomatoes, cut up; and 1 teaspoon chili powder. Turn into 2-quart casserole. Bake, uncovered, at 350° for 30 minutes. Sprinkle 4 ounces American cheese, shredded (1 cup), atop. Bake 3 minutes to melt cheese. Serves 6.

VEGETABLE-MEAT MEDLEY

- 1 pound bulk pork sausage*
- ¼ cup chopped onion
- 3 tablespoons all-purpose flour
- 1 16-ounce can tomatoes, cut up
- 1 8¾-ounce can whole kernel corn
- 1 8-ounce can cut green beans
- 1 cup sifted all-purpose flour
- 1½ teaspoons baking powder
- ½ teaspoon dry mustard
- 2 tablespoons shortening
- ⅔ cup milk
- 3 ounces sharp process American cheese, shredded (¾ cup)

In skillet cook meat with onion till meat is brown and onion is tender, breaking up meat as it cooks. Drain off excess fat. Blend in 3 tablespoons flour, ¼ teaspoon salt, and dash pepper. Stir in tomatoes and cook till slightly thickened. Drain corn and beans; add vegetables to meat mixture. Heat to boiling; spoon into 4 individual casseroles.

Meanwhile, sift together 1 cup flour, baking powder, ½ teaspoon salt, and mustard. Cut in shortening; blend in milk and ½ *cup* of the cheese to form soft dough. Drop biscuit dough onto *boiling hot* mixture. Sprinkle with remaining ¼ cup cheese. Bake, uncovered, at 350° for 30 minutes, till brown. Serves 4.

*Or, substitute ground beef for sausage and increase salt in meat mixture to ¾ teaspoon.

MINESTRONE BAKE

In skillet brown 1 pound ground pork and ½ cup chopped onion. Drain off excess fat. Stir in one 10¾-ounce can condensed minestrone soup; one 10½-ounce can condensed cream of mushroom soup; one 8-ounce can cut green beans, drained; 3 medium raw potatoes, peeled and cubed (3 cups); and 1 cup milk. Turn into 2-quart casserole. Bake, covered, at 350° for 1 hour. Uncover; bake 30 to 45 minutes or till potatoes are done. Serves 6.

Ground meat casseroles are as American → as the Fourth of July. Vegetable-Meat Medley sports a biscuit topper and uses either pork sausage or ground beef.

CHOW MEIN BEEF BAKE

1 pound ground beef
1 cup bias-sliced celery
½ cup chopped onion
1 medium tomato, peeled
   and diced
1 3-ounce can sliced mushrooms,
   drained (½ cup)
1 10½-ounce can condensed cream
   of mushroom soup
1 3-ounce can chow mein noodles

In large skillet combine beef, celery, and onion. Cook till meat is lightly browned; drain off excess fat. Add tomato, mushrooms, soup, ½ cup water, and *half* of the chow mein noodles; stir till blended. Turn into 1½-quart casserole; top with remaining noodles. Bake at 350° for 30 minutes. Pass soy sauce, if desired. Makes 4 or 5 servings.

EGGPLANT AND BEEF BAKE

1 large or 2 small eggplants
1 beaten egg
½ cup milk
2 cups soft bread cubes
   (2 slices)
1 tablespoon snipped parsley
¼ teaspoon dried basil leaves,
   crushed
1 pound ground beef
   • • •
1 beaten egg
2 tablespoons shortening
1 8-ounce can tomato sauce
¼ cup water

Cut each eggplant into 10 to 12 slices, ¼ inch thick. (Peel if desired.) Sprinkle with salt. Combine 1 beaten egg, milk, bread cubes, parsley, ½ teaspoon salt, and basil. Add meat; mix well. Spread mixture on *half* of the eggplant slices; top with remaining slices.

   Combine 1 beaten egg and 2 tablespoons water; dip eggplant "sandwiches" in egg mixture. Brown on both sides in hot shortening. Transfer to 12x7½x2-inch baking dish overlapping pieces to fit. Combine tomato sauce and water; pour over eggplant. Bake at 350° for 35 to 40 minutes. Serves 5 or 6.

BEEF AND GREEN BEANS

1 pound ground beef
1 9-ounce package frozen French-
   style green beans, cooked
   and drained
1 10½-ounce can condensed cream
   of celery soup
1 3-ounce can chopped mushrooms,
   drained (½ cup)
½ cup dairy sour cream
⅛ teaspoon dried thyme leaves,
   crushed
   Dash pepper
¼ cup fine dry bread crumbs
2 tablespoons butter or margarine,
   melted

Brown meat in skillet; drain off excess fat. Stir in beans, soup, mushrooms, sour cream, thyme, and pepper. Pour into 1½-quart casserole. Combine bread crumbs with melted butter. Sprinkle over casserole. Bake at 350° for 40 to 45 minutes or till heated through. Makes 6 servings.

LAMB SOUFFLE

Ground beef or veal can be substituted for lamb—

1 pound ground lamb
2 tablespoons salad oil
1 10½-ounce can condensed cream
   of mushroom soup
⅔ cup milk
¼ teaspoon Worcestershire sauce
½ cup fine dry bread crumbs
3 well-beaten egg yolks
2 tablespoons snipped parsley
1 tablespoon finely chopped onion
3 stiff-beaten egg whites

In saucepan crumble and brown lamb in hot salad oil. Drain off excess fat. Combine soup, milk, and Worcestershire sauce. Add 1 *cup* soup mixture to meat; reserve remaining soup mixture for the sauce. Stir in bread crumbs, egg yolks, parsley, and onion. Fold in stiff-beaten egg whites. Pour into greased 1-quart casserole. Bake at 350° for 45 to 50 minutes. Heat remaining soup mixture; serve with souffle. Makes 4 servings.

MACARONI-BEEF CASSEROLE

1 cup uncooked elbow macaroni
1 8-ounce can tomato sauce
2 eggs
¼ cup finely chopped onion
1 tablespoon snipped parsley
1 teaspoon salt
1 teaspoon Worcestershire sauce
¼ teaspoon ground sage
⅛ teaspoon pepper
½ cup whole bran cereal
1½ pounds ground beef

Cook macaroni according to package directions; drain. Combine tomato sauce, eggs, onion, parsley, salt, Worcestershire sauce, sage, and pepper. Add cereal; beat well with rotary beater. Add ground beef; mix well. Stir in cooked macaroni.

Press lightly into 2-quart casserole. Bake, uncovered, at 375° for 1 hour. Remove from oven; let stand 5 minutes. Loosen sides; invert dish onto platter and unmold. Trim with parsley, if desired. Makes 8 servings.

ENCHILADA CASSEROLE

Adjust the "hotness" by adding the desired amount of chopped green chilies—

6 tortillas (frozen or canned)
  Salad oil
1 pound ground beef
½ cup chopped onion
1 10½-ounce can condensed cream of mushroom soup
1 10-ounce can enchilada sauce
1 6-ounce can evaporated milk
4 ounces sharp process American cheese, shredded (1 cup)
2 to 4 tablespoons canned green chilies, seeded and chopped

Fry tortillas in hot salad oil until crisp according to label directions. Drain. Break in bite-size pieces. Cook beef and onion in skillet till meat is lightly browned. Stir in soup. Add remaining ingredients and tortillas. Turn into 2-quart casserole. Bake at 350° for 1 hour. Stir once or twice while baking. Makes 6 servings.

ZUCCHINI-BEEF BAKE

6 small zucchini (1½ pounds)
1 pound ground beef
½ cup chopped onion
1½ cups soft bread crumbs (about 2 slices)
¼ teaspoon dried thyme leaves, crushed
¼ cup butter or margarine
¼ cup all-purpose flour
2 cups milk
4 ounces sharp process American cheese, shredded (1 cup)
1 tablespoon butter, melted

Wash and remove ends from zucchini; cut in ½-inch slices. Cook in boiling salted water for 5 minutes or till tender; drain. In skillet cook meat with onion till meat is brown; drain off excess fat. Stir in ½ *cup* bread crumbs, ¾ teaspoon salt, thyme, and ⅛ teaspoon pepper. Remove from heat.

In saucepan melt ¼ cup butter; blend in flour and ½ teaspoon salt. Add milk all at once. Cook and stir till mixture thickens and bubbles. Add cheese; stir till melted. Stir in meat mixture. Place *half* of zucchini in 2-quart baking dish; pour *half* of the cheese mixture atop. Repeat layers. Combine remaining bread crumbs with 1 tablespoon melted butter. Sprinkle atop casserole. Bake at 350° for 30 to 35 minutes. Serves 6.

BISCUIT HAMBURGER BAKE

In skillet cook 1½ pounds ground beef and ½ cup chopped onion till meat is brown. Drain off fat. Stir in one 10½-ounce can condensed cream of celery soup; ⅓ cup milk; ½ teaspoon dried oregano leaves, crushed; and dash pepper. Heat to boiling. Turn into 8¼x 1¾-inch round ovenware cake dish.

To prepare biscuit, add ½ cup milk to 1 cup packaged biscuit mix. Stir with a fork forming a soft dough; beat 15 strokes. Spread over *hot* meat mixture. Bake at 450° for 15 minutes or till biscuit topping is browned. Spread biscuit with ½ cup dairy sour cream. Sprinkle with 1 tablespoon shredded Parmesan cheese and a little snipped parsley. Bake 2 minutes longer. Makes 6 servings.

Dunk refrigerated biscuits in melted butter and then in yellow cornmeal to make a crunchy topping for Western Casserole.

WESTERN CASSEROLE

1 pound ground beef
1 16-ounce can whole kernel corn, drained
1 16-ounce can red kidney beans, drained
1 10¾-ounce can condensed tomato soup
4 ounces sharp process American cheese, shredded (1 cup)
¼ cup milk
1 teaspoon instant minced onion
½ teaspoon chili powder
. . .
1 package refrigerated biscuits (10 biscuits)
2 tablespoons butter or margarine, melted
¼ cup yellow cornmeal

Brown beef in skillet. Stir in corn, kidney beans, tomato soup, cheese, milk, onion, and chili powder; bring to boiling. Turn boiling mixture into 2-quart casserole. Bake, uncovered, at 400° for 10 minutes.

Dip the refrigerated biscuits in melted butter or margarine, then in cornmeal. Place around edge of *boiling hot* casserole mixture. Bake 20 minutes longer, or till biscuits are golden. Makes 5 or 6 servings.

BEEF AND NOODLES

1 5½-ounce package noodles with sour cream-cheese sauce mix
1 pound ground beef
½ cup chopped onion
1 10½-ounce can condensed cream of mushroom soup
½ cup milk
2 tablespoons chopped canned pimiento
¼ teaspoon dried thyme leaves, crushed
Dash pepper
1 cup soft bread crumbs
2 tablespoons butter, melted
2 ounces sharp Cheddar cheese, shredded (½ cup)

Prepare noodles with sauce mix according to package directions. Brown meat and onion in skillet. Stir in soup, milk, pimiento, thyme, and pepper. Add cooked noodle mixture. Turn into 10x6x1½-inch baking dish. Combine crumbs and butter. Sprinkle atop casserole. Bake at 350° for 30 minutes. Sprinkle with cheese; bake 5 minutes longer. Serves 6.

EASY MEXICALI DINNER

1 pound ground beef
1 medium onion, chopped
6 ounces medium noodles, cooked and drained
1 16-ounce can tomatoes, cut up
1 6-ounce can tomato paste
4 ounces sharp process American cheese, shredded (1 cup)
½ cup sliced pitted ripe olives
1 teaspoon salt
¼ teaspoon dried basil leaves, crushed
⅛ teaspoon pepper
2 ounces sharp process American cheese, shredded (½ cup)

Brown beef in skillet. Add onion and cook till tender. Stir in cooked noodles, tomatoes, tomato paste, 1 cup cheese, olives, and seasonings. Turn into 2-quart casserole. Top with the ½ cup cheese. Bake, uncovered, at 350° for 45 minutes or till hot. Serves 6.

SIX-LAYER DINNER

It's simple to put together—

> 3 cups sliced, peeled, raw
>   potatoes
> 1 17-ounce can whole kernel corn,
>   drained
> 1 medium onion, sliced
> 1 pound ground beef
> 1 cup sliced raw carrots
> 1½ teaspoons salt
> ⅛ teaspoon pepper
> 1 16-ounce can tomatoes, cut up

Layer potatoes, corn, onion, meat, and carrots in 3-quart casserole, seasoning each layer with salt and pepper. Pour tomatoes over top. Cover and bake at 350° for 1¾ hours, or till vegetables are done. Makes 6 servings.

PORK AND SPAGHETTI BAKE

Use leftover roast pork in this tempting dish—

> 4 ounces spaghetti, broken
> 1 cup chopped celery
> ½ cup chopped onion
> ¼ cup butter or margarine
> 1 10¾-ounce can condensed
>   Cheddar cheese soup
> ¾ cup milk
> 2 tablespoons grated Parmesan
>   cheese
> ½ teaspoon dry mustard
> 2 cups ground cooked roast pork
> 1 8-ounce can cut green beans,
>   drained
> ¼ cup chopped canned pimiento
> ½ cup crisp rice cereal, crushed
> 1 tablespoon butter, melted

Cook spaghetti in boiling salted water following package directions; drain. In large saucepan cook celery and onion in ¼ cup butter till crisp-tender. Blend in soup, milk, Parmesan cheese, and dry mustard. Stir in pork, beans, and pimiento; mix well. Toss meat mixture with cooked spaghetti. Turn into 1½-quart casserole. Mix cereal with melted butter and sprinkle over top. Bake, uncovered, at 350° for 45 to 50 minutes. Serves 6 to 8.

CHEESEBURGER CASSEROLE

> 8 ounces wide noodles
> 1½ pounds ground beef
> ½ cup chopped onion
> 1 15-ounce can tomato sauce
> 1 3-ounce can (⅔ cup) chopped
>   mushrooms, undrained
> 1 8-ounce package sliced sharp
>   process American cheese
>   (8 slices)

Cook noodles according to package directions; drain. In large skillet brown beef and onion. Stir in ¾ teaspoon salt, dash pepper, cooked noodles, tomato sauce, undrained mushrooms, and *4 slices* of the cheese, cut up. Turn into 13x9x2-inch baking dish. Bake, uncovered, at 350° for 35 minutes. Arrange remaining 4 slices cheese over top; return to oven till cheese melts. Serves 8 to 10.

HAMBURGER PIE

> 1 pound ground beef
> ½ cup chopped onion
> 1 16-ounce can cut green beans,
>   drained
> 1 10¾-ounce can condensed tomato
>   soup
> 5 medium cooked, peeled, potatoes*
> ½ cup warm milk
> 1 beaten egg
> 2 ounces process American cheese,
>   shredded (½ cup), optional

In skillet combine meat, onion, ½ teaspoon salt, and dash pepper. Brown meat lightly. Add drained green beans and condensed soup. Turn into 1½-quart casserole.

Mash potatoes while hot; add milk and egg. Season with salt and pepper. Drop in mounds over meat. Sprinkle potatoes with shredded cheese. Bake, uncovered, at 350° for 25 to 30 minutes. Makes 6 servings.

*For speed omit the cooked potatoes and use packaged instant mashed potatoes. Prepare enough instant mashed potatoes for 4 servings according to package directions, but *reserve the milk*. Add egg to potatoes. Season with salt and pepper. Slowly add enough reserved milk to make potatoes hold shape.

CHEESY BEEF PIE

- 1 pound ground beef
- ½ cup chopped onion
- 1 8-ounce can tomato sauce
- ¼ cup snipped parsley
- 1 3-ounce can chopped mushrooms, drained (½ cup)
- ¼ teaspoon dried oregano leaves, crushed
- 2 packages refrigerated crescent rolls (8 rolls in each)
- 3 eggs
- 6 slices sharp process American cheese

In skillet brown beef and onion; drain. Stir in next 4 ingredients and ⅛ teaspoon pepper; set aside. Unroll *one* package of rolls. Place the four sections of dough together, forming 12x6-inch rectangle. Seal edges and perforations together. Roll to 12-inch square. Fit into 9-inch pie plate; trim.

Separate *one* of the eggs; set yolk aside. Beat egg white with remaining *two* eggs. Spread *half* over dough. Spoon meat into shell. Arrange cheese slices atop; spread remaining egg mixture over cheese. Mix reserved yolk and 1 tablespoon water; brush lightly on edge of pastry. Reserve remaining.

Roll second package of rolls to 12-inch square as before. Place atop filling. Trim, seal, and flute edge; cut slits for escape of steam. Brush top with remaining egg yolk mixture. Bake at 350° for 50 to 55 minutes. If pastry gets too brown, cover with foil. Let stand 10 minutes. Makes 6 servings.

PIZZA MEAT PIE

Combine one 6-ounce can evaporated milk, ½ cup fine dry bread crumbs, and ¼ to ½ teaspoon garlic salt. Add 1 pound ground beef; mix well. Press mixture into bottom and sides of 9-inch pie plate. Spread ½ cup catsup over meat. Sprinkle with ½ teaspoon dried oregano leaves, crushed, and one 3-ounce can sliced mushrooms, drained. Top with ¾ cup shredded sharp process American cheese. Bake at 375° for 15 minutes. Sprinkle with 2 tablespoons grated Parmesan cheese. Bake 5 minutes longer. Makes 4 to 6 servings.

MEAT AND POTATO PIE

- 1 beaten egg
- ½ cup milk
- ¾ cup soft bread crumbs (about 1 slice)
- ¾ teaspoon salt
  - Dash pepper
- 1 pound ground beef
  - • • •
- 3 cups diced, cooked potatoes
- ⅓ cup chili sauce
- ¼ cup chopped green onion
- 1 teaspoon prepared mustard
- ½ teaspoon salt
- 2 ounces sharp process American cheese, shredded (½ cup)

Combine first 5 ingredients; add beef and mix well. Press mixture into bottom and sides of 9-inch pie plate. Combine potatoes, chili sauce, onion, mustard, and salt; toss lightly. Spread in meat shell. Bake at 350° for 35 minutes. Remove from oven; sprinkle with cheese. Return to oven till cheese melts, about 3 minutes. Makes 6 servings.

GROUND LAMB PIE

Prepare enough packaged instant mashed potatoes for 4 servings according to package directions, *except omit the salt.*

In skillet cook 1 pound ground lamb, ½ cup finely chopped celery, and 2 tablespoons chopped onion till meat is browned and vegetables are tender. Stir in 2 tablespoons all-purpose flour. Add 1 cup milk all at once. Cook and stir till mixture thickens and bubbles. Stir in 1 tablespoon snipped parsley, ¾ teaspoon salt, ¼ teaspoon dried dillweed, and ¼ teaspoon kitchen bouquet.

Spread meat mixture in 1½-quart casserole. Top evenly with potatoes. Sprinkle with ¼ cup shredded sharp process American cheese. Bake at 400° for 20 to 25 minutes, or till brown. Makes 6 servings.

Don't shy away from main dish pies because of the piecrust. The crust for Cheesy Beef Pie is a snap to prepare. It's made from refrigerated crescent rolls.

Burger in the Round is a real palate-teaser. It tastes like a stuffed green pepper, only this version is inside-out with a green pepper layer in the center.

BURGER IN THE ROUND

Combine 1 beaten egg, ¾ cup milk, ¾ cup soft bread crumbs (about 1 slice), ½ cup chopped onion, 1 teaspoon salt, and dash pepper. Add 1½ pounds ground beef and mix thoroughly. Pat *half* the meat mixture into 8¼x1¾-inch round ovenware cake dish.

Cook 1 cup coarsely chopped green pepper and 1 clove garlic, minced, in 1 tablespoon butter or margarine till green pepper is crisp-tender. Spread over meat mixture layer. Top green pepper mixture with remaining meat mixture, spreading evenly.

Bake at 350° for 35 minutes. Pour ¼ cup bottled barbecue sauce over meat. Garnish top with green pepper triangles, if desired. Return to oven and bake 10 minutes longer. To serve, cut in wedges. Makes 6 servings.

HAMBURGER-ONION PIE

Prepare 1 package pie crust mix following package directions for 2-crust pie. Using about ½ the pastry, line 9-inch pie plate; set remaining pastry aside for top crust. In skillet cook 1½ cups thinly sliced onion and ¼ cup chopped green pepper in ¼ cup butter till tender. Add 1 pound ground beef; brown. Drain off fat. Stir in 2 tablespoons all-purpose flour, ¾ teaspoon salt, and ⅛ teaspoon pepper; cook 2 minutes. Remove from heat.

Combine 1 well-beaten egg, 1 cup dairy sour cream, 2 tablespoons snipped parsley, and 2 tablespoons chopped canned pimiento. Add to meat mixture; mix well. Turn into pastry-lined pie plate. Adjust top crust; cut slits for escape of steam. Bake at 375° for 40 minutes or till lightly browned. Serves 6.

HAM IN CHEESE CRUST

1½ cups finely crushed round
    cheese crackers (about 36)
6 tablespoons butter or margarine,
    melted
2 beaten eggs
1 6-ounce can (⅔ cup) evaporated
    milk
¼ cup finely chopped onion
¼ cup finely chopped green pepper
1 tablespoon prepared mustard
1 teaspoon prepared horseradish
1 pound ground fully-cooked ham

For crust, mix cracker crumbs and butter. Reserving 2 tablespoons crumb mixture, press remaining on bottom and sides of 9-inch pie plate. Bake at 350° for 10 minutes.

Meanwhile, combine eggs, evaporated milk, onion, green pepper, mustard, and horseradish. Add ham; mix well. Turn into baked crumb crust. Bake at 350° for 35 minutes. Sprinkle with reserved crumbs; bake 5 to 10 minutes longer. Let stand 5 minutes before cutting into wedges. Makes 6 servings.

Entice the family with a meat pie that combines the familiar ham and cheese

HAM UPSIDE-DOWN PIE

½ cup uncooked long-grain rice
2 beaten eggs
¼ cup chopped onion
1 tablespoon snipped parsley
1 pound ground fully-cooked ham
    (3 cups)
. . .
¼ cup chili sauce
2 tablespoons brown sugar
1 tablespoon prepared mustard
1 8½-ounce can sliced pineapple

Cook rice according to package directions. Combine eggs, cooked rice, onion, and parsley. Add ham; mix thoroughly. Combine chili sauce, brown sugar, and mustard.

Drain pineapple, reserving 2 tablespoons syrup. Add reserved pineapple syrup to chili sauce mixture. Halve pineapple slices and arrange on bottom of 10-inch pie plate. Pour chili sauce mixture over pineapple. Press ham mixture atop pineapple. Bake at 350° for 50 to 55 minutes. Invert on serving platter. Cut in wedges to serve. Serves 5 or 6.

flavor in an unusual way. Serve Ham in Cheese Crust for dinner, tonight.

WHEN COMPANY COMES TO DINNER

Dress up ground meat and entertain company on a budget. By adding special ingredients, such as wine, and by shaping the meat in a special way, ground meat is taken out of the everyday class and elevated to company fare for entertaining.

Create interesting appetizers with ground meat. Appetizer meatballs that are dipped in a sauce or actually cooked fondue-style can be the hit of many parties, as can dips, spreads, and tidbits concocted with various ground meats.

And check the Cooking for a Crowd section for appealing ideas to feed hungry mouths at a family reunion or church supper. Also included are tips for menu planning and buffet service.

Company-best Planked Meat Loaf, flanked with grilled tomatoes, presents meat and vegetables elegantly.

Appetizers
for Entertaining

BULL'S-EYE MEATBALLS

10 slices white bread
    Butter or margarine, softened
1 pound ground beef
2 tablespoons grated onion
1 tablespoon Worcestershire sauce
1 teaspoon salt
    Chili sauce

With 1½-inch cutter, cut 4 rounds from each slice of bread. Toast rounds on one side; butter untoasted side. Combine meat and next 3 ingredients; mix well. Shape into 40 balls; make an indentation in top of each ball. Place balls on buttered rounds. Broil 4 inches from heat 5 to 6 minutes. Fill centers with chili sauce. Serve hot. Makes 40.

APPETIZER TIPS

Palate-tempting morsels can spark the party and keep guests circulating. Vary the scene with hot as well as cold tidbits. Hot appetizers needn't imply a kitchen-bound hostess. Utilize chafing dishes and hot trays to keep them hot. If foods must be served from the oven, stagger their appearance. Do as much pre-preparation as possible, then heat as needed. Guests will savor the aroma of fresh hot appetizers and marvel at the successful hostess.

APPETIZER MEATBALLS

¼ cup milk
2 tablespoons fine dry bread
    crumbs
1 tablespoon finely chopped onion
½ pound ground beef
2 tablespoons water
2 tablespoons soy sauce
1 tablespoon salad oil
2 teaspoons sugar
½ clove garlic, crushed
¼ teaspoon ground ginger

Combine first 3 ingredients. Add meat; mix well. Shape into 3 dozen small balls. Place in shallow baking pan. Blend remaining ingredients. Pour over meatballs. Let stand 1 hour, stirring once or twice. Bake meatballs in sauce, uncovered, at 350° for 20 to 25 minutes. Serve hot in chafing dish. Makes 36.

GLAZED SAUSAGE TIDBITS

1 beaten egg
⅛ cup milk
½ cup finely crushed saltine
    cracker crumbs (14 crackers)
½ teaspoon ground sage
1 pound bulk pork sausage
2 tablespoons brown sugar
1 teaspoon cornstarch
¼ cup catsup
1 tablespoon vinegar
1 tablespoon soy sauce

Combine first 4 ingredients. Add sausage; mix well. Shape into 3 dozen small balls. In skillet brown balls slowly on all sides, about 15 minutes. Pour off fat. Blend brown sugar with cornstarch. Add ½ cup cold water and remaining ingredients. Pour over balls. Cover; simmer 15 minutes, stirring often. Serve hot in chafing dish. Makes 3 dozen.

MINIATURE LAMB BALLS

1 beaten egg
⅓ cup fine dry bread crumbs
¼ cup applesauce
½ pound ground lamb
¼ cup bottled mint sauce

Combine first 3 ingredients, ½ teaspoon salt, and dash pepper. Add lamb; mix well. Shape into 30 small balls. Place in shallow baking pan. Bake at 375° for 15 minutes. Meanwhile, heat mint sauce. Serve meatballs in chafing dish; pour sauce over. Makes 30 meatballs.

COCKTAIL HAM NUGGETS

1 beaten egg
1 tablespoon milk
1 5-ounce can water chestnuts, drained and finely chopped
¼ cup chopped green onion with tops
1 small clove garlic, crushed
½ pound ground fully-cooked ham
½ pound ground pork
Shortening

Combine first 5 ingredients. Add meats and mix well. Using about 2 teaspoons mixture for each, form into marble-size meatballs. Brown slowly on all sides in small amount of hot shortening. Continue cooking till done, shaking skillet to turn meatballs. Serve with wooden picks. Makes about 5 dozen.

Entice guests to help themselves to zippy Cocktail Ham Nuggets spiked with green onion and crunchy water chestnuts.

STUFFED MUSHROOM BITES

Use canned mushrooms if fresh aren't available—

2 dozen fresh medium mushrooms
   or two 6-ounce cans whole mushrooms, drained
½ teaspoon instant minced onion
1 teaspoon butter or margarine
½ cup ground fully-cooked ham
1 teaspoon chopped green pepper
½ teaspoon prepared mustard
¼ teaspoon Worcestershire sauce
1 drop bottled hot pepper sauce
¼ cup soft bread crumbs
2 tablespoons milk

Carefully remove mushroom stems.* Finely chop stems; cook with onion in butter till tender but not brown. Remove from heat. Stir in ham and next 4 ingredients. Combine crumbs and milk. Add to ham; mix well.

Mound stuffing in mushrooms using about 2 teaspoons filling for each fresh mushroom or 1 teaspoon filling for each canned mushroom. Place on baking sheet. Bake at 400° for 10 to 12 minutes till fresh mushrooms are tender or canned mushrooms are hot. Makes 2 dozen fresh mushroom appetizers *or* about 3 dozen canned mushroom appetizers.

*For fresh mushrooms, wash and trim off tips of stems. If extra large, pour boiling water over caps; let stand for 1 minute. Drain.

HAM-PRETZEL TEASERS

Eat the pretzel stick along with the meatball—

1 3-ounce package cream cheese, softened
1 cup ground fully-cooked ham
¼ cup chopped pecans
¼ teaspoon Worcestershire sauce
   Several drops onion juice
½ cup finely snipped parsley
   Thin pretzel sticks

Blend cream cheese, ham, pecans, Worcestershire sauce, and onion juice; chill. Shape mixture into 3 dozen small balls. Chill till serving time. Insert pretzel stick into each ball. Roll sides in parsley. Makes 3 dozen.

For **Hurry-up Ham Puffs:** Have bakery cut 1 unsliced sandwich loaf bread into lengthwise slices ½ inch thick. In broiler toast 3 slices on both sides. Store remaining slices. Halve 15 small pimiento-stuffed green olives. Set aside.

Mix 1½ cups ground fully-cooked ham, ⅓ cup mayonnaise, 2 tablespoons finely chopped onion, 1 teaspoon prepared mustard, and ½ teaspoon prepared horseradish; spread on toasted slices.

Arrange 10 olive halves atop each slice. Blend ½ cup mayonnaise with ½ teaspoon dry mustard; fold into 3 stiff-beaten egg whites. Mound mixture atop olives. Bake at 400° for 10 to 12 minutes. Cut each slice into 10. Serve hot. Makes 30.

BEEF PUFF APPETIZERS

Miniature cream puffs filled with ground beef and cheese make the perfect hot appetizer—

    2 tablespoons butter or margarine
    ¼ cup all-purpose flour
    1 egg
    ¼ cup shredded process Swiss cheese
    ¼ pound ground beef
    2 tablespoons chopped onion
    1 tablespoon all-purpose flour
    1 tablespoon pickle relish
    2 or 3 drops bottled hot pepper sauce

In saucepan melt 2 tablespoons butter in ¼ cup boiling water. Add ¼ cup flour and dash salt all at once; stir vigorously. Cook and stir till mixture forms a ball that doesn't separate. Remove from heat; cool slightly.

Add egg and beat vigorously till smooth. Stir in cheese. Using 1 level measuring teaspoon dough for each cream puff, drop dough onto greased baking sheet. Bake at 400° for 20 minutes. Remove from oven; cool. Split, cutting off tops about ⅓ of the way down.

Meanwhile, in small saucepan cook meat with onion till meat is browned and onion is tender. Blend in 1 tablespoon flour. Add ¼ cup water, pickle relish, ⅛ teaspoon salt, and hot pepper sauce. Cook, stirring constantly, till mixture thickens and bubbles. Spoon about 1 teaspoon mixture into each cream puff. Serve hot. Makes 2½ dozen appetizers.

HOT CHICKEN SPREAD

    2 cups coarsely ground cooked chicken
    ½ cup ground almonds
    ½ cup mayonnaise or salad dressing
    ¼ teaspoon curry powder
      Assorted crackers, melba toast rounds, or potato chips
      Paprika

Blend first 4 ingredients and salt to taste. Spread on crackers, toast, or chips. Sprinkle with paprika; place on baking sheet. Bake at 400° for 3 minutes. Makes 2 cups.

TURKEY APPETIZER BALL

1 cup ground cooked turkey
4 slices bacon, crisp-cooked
   and crumbled
½ cup dairy sour cream
2 tablespoons crumbled blue cheese
⅓ cup chopped pecans

Combine turkey, bacon, sour cream, and blue cheese. Chill. Form into ball. Roll in nuts. Serve with crackers. Makes 1 cup.

DEVILED GUACAMOLE

2 avocados, pitted and peeled
1 cup ground fully-cooked ham
1 to 2 tablespoons finely chopped
   canned green chilies, seeded
1 tablespoon lemon juice
1 teaspoon grated onion

Mash avocados with fork. Stir in remaining ingredients; chill. Serve with corn chips and assorted crackers. Makes 1½ cups.

BRANDIED LIVER PATE

¼ cup chopped onion
½ small clove garlic, crushed
1 tablespoon butter or margarine
1 8-ounce package chicken livers
2 tablespoons butter or margarine
1 teaspoon all-purpose flour
⅛ teaspoon dried oregano leaves,
   crushed
⅛ teaspoon celery salt
2 teaspoons brandy

Cook onion and garlic in 1 tablespoon butter till tender. Remove from skillet. In same skillet cook livers, covered, in 2 tablespoons butter over low heat till no longer pink. Add flour, ¼ teaspoon salt, oregano, celery salt, and dash pepper. Cook and stir over low heat for 1 minute. Add onion and brandy. Turn into blender container and blend till smooth, or put through meat grinder several times. Mold in small bowl. Chill several hours. Unmold. Garnish with chopped hard-cooked egg, if desired. Makes 1 cup.

HOT SAUSAGE-BEAN DIP

Use blender for a smooth dip—

½ pound bulk pork sausage
1 16-ounce can pork and beans
   in tomato sauce
2 ounces sharp process American
   cheese, shredded (½ cup)
2 tablespoons catsup
½ teaspoon prepared mustard
   Few drops bottled hot pepper
   sauce

In skillet break sausage into small pieces. Cook slowly until browned, about 10 minutes. Drain off fat. In blender combine sausage with beans, shredded cheese, catsup, mustard, and hot pepper sauce; blend till smooth, stopping occasionally to scrape down sides. Return to skillet. Heat. Serve with corn chips or assorted crackers. Makes 2½ cups.

ZIPPY HAM DIP

Horseradish adds zip—

Beat two 3-ounce packages cream cheese, softened, with ⅓ cup milk till light and creamy. Stir in 1½ cups ground fully-cooked ham; 2 tablespoons finely chopped green pepper; and 1 tablespoon prepared horseradish. Cover; chill. Serve with potato chips, assorted crackers, or corn chips. Makes 2 cups.

HAM PATE

1 beaten egg
¼ cup milk
¼ cup finely chopped onion
2 tablespoons catsup
4 teaspoons prepared mustard
4 to 5 drops bottled hot pepper
   sauce
1½ cups ground fully-cooked ham

Combine first 6 ingredients; add ham and mix well. Pack into greased 5½x3x2¼-inch loaf pan. Bake at 325° for 1 hour. Cool, then unmold onto serving plate. Chill. Serve cold with assorted crackers. Makes 1¾ cups.

SURPRISE MEATBALLS

  1 beaten egg
  ⅔ cup soft bread crumbs
  2 tablespoons finely chopped onion
  ½ teaspoon Worcestershire sauce
  ½ pound ground beef
    Pimiento-stuffed green olives
    Cocktail onions
    Canned pineapple tidbits
    Canned whole mushrooms
    Tangy Cocktail Dip

Combine first 4 ingredients and ¼ teaspoon salt. Add meat; mix well. Drain olives, onions, pineapple, and mushrooms. Halve pineapple tidbits and larger mushrooms. Shape meat around each olive, onion, pineapple, or mushroom. Place on shallow baking pan. Bake at 425° for 10 minutes. Serve hot on cocktail picks with *Tangy Cocktail Dip:* Combine 1 cup catsup; 4 teaspoons brown sugar; 4 teaspoons prepared mustard; and 6 drops bottled hot pepper sauce. Heat. Makes 3 dozen.

BEEF BALL DIPPERS

  1 beaten egg
  ⅓ cup soft bread crumbs
  ¼ cup finely chopped onion
  ¼ teaspoon salt
  1 pound ground beef
  1 cup dairy sour cream
  2 tablespoons all-purpose flour
  1 beef bouillon cube

Combine first 4 ingredients. Add beef; mix well. Shape into 4 dozen balls. Place in 15½x 10½x1-inch baking pan. Bake at 400° for 15 minutes, shaking pan to turn balls.

    In saucepan blend sour cream with flour. Dissolve bouillon cube in 1 cup boiling water; gradually stir into sour cream. Cook and stir over medium-low heat till bubbly; cook and stir 1 minute more. Serve as dip with meatballs. Makes 4 dozen appetizers.

← Liven appetites and conversation at the next party with Surprise Meatballs. An assortment of sweet and tangy centers makes each meatball a tasty morsel.

MEATBALL FONDUE

  1 tablespoon soy sauce
  2 teaspoons sugar
  ¼ teaspoon instant minced onion
    Dash garlic salt
    Dash ground ginger
  ½ pound ground beef
  ½ cup fine soft bread crumbs
    Salad oil

Combine first 5 ingredients and 1 tablespoon water; let stand 10 minutes. Combine beef and crumbs. Add soy mixture; mix well. Shape into 30 meatballs. Spear on bamboo skewers; cook in deep hot fat (375°) in fondue pot 1½ minutes. Serve mustard or catsup, if desired, for dipping. Makes 30 appetizers.

CURRIED COCKTAIL BITES

  1 beaten egg
  ½ cup milk
  ⅔ cup soft bread crumbs
  2 tablespoons grated onion
  1 pound ground beef
  2 tablespoons salad oil
  1 10½-ounce can condensed
    cream of mushroom soup
  ¼ cup dry sherry
  ½ teaspoon curry powder

Combine first 4 ingredients and ½ teaspoon salt. Add beef; mix well. Shape into 60 small balls. In skillet brown balls, a single layer at a time, in hot oil, shaking skillet to turn balls. Cook slowly 5 minutes. Repeat with remaining balls. Combine last 3 ingredients; heat. Serve as dip with meatballs. Makes 60.

TINY CHEESEBURGERS

    Combine ½ pound ground beef, 2 tablespoons chopped onion, ½ teaspoon dried dillweed, and ¼ teaspoon salt; mix well. Spread on sliced party rye bread *or* shredded wheat wafers. Cut sliced process Swiss cheese into squares to fit bread slices or wafers. Place cheese atop each appetizer. Place on shallow baking pan. Bake at 400° for 8 to 10 minutes. Serve hot. Makes about 20 appetizers.

Meat Dishes
for the Gourmet

MEATBALLS A LA BURGUNDY

    1 beaten egg
    ½ cup milk
    ⅓ cup quick-cooking rolled oats
    ¼ cup finely chopped onion
    1 pound ground beef
    2 tablespoons shortening
    ¼ cup all-purpose flour
    ½ cup red Burgundy
    2 beef bouillon cubes
    1 teaspoon sugar
    1 teaspoon kitchen bouquet

Combine first 4 ingredients and ½ teaspoon salt. Add beef; mix well. Shape into 24 balls; brown in hot shortening in skillet. Remove balls; reserve drippings in skillet. Stir flour into reserved drippings. Add 2 cups water, wine, and bouillon cubes; cook and stir till bubbly. Stir in remaining ingredients; add balls. Cover; simmer 20 minutes. Serves 6.

HAMBURGER STEAK DIANE

    1½ pounds ground round or sirloin
    1 teaspoon dry mustard
    2 tablespoons butter or margarine
    1 to 2 tablespoons lemon juice
    1 tablespoon snipped parsley
    ½ teaspoon Worcestershire sauce
    ¼ cup brandy, optional

Combine meat, mustard, 1 teaspoon salt, and dash pepper; mix well. Shape into 5 patties, ½ inch thick. Melt butter in blazer pan of chafing dish over direct flame or in skillet over medium-high heat. Cook meat 2 minutes on each side; remove. To blazer pan add lemon juice, parsley, and Worcestershire; bring to boiling. Reduce heat. In saucepan heat brandy over very low heat. Add to sauce; ignite. Serve at once over meat. Serves 5.

HAM-STUFFED POTATOES

    4 large baking potatoes
    2 cups ground fully-cooked ham
    1 cup mayonnaise or salad dressing
    2 ounces process Swiss cheese,
        shredded (½ cup)
    2 tablespoons chopped green pepper
    2 tablespoons chopped canned
        pimiento
    1 tablespoon instant minced onion
    1 ounce process American cheese,
        shredded (¼ cup)

Scrub potatoes. Bake at 425° for 45 to 60 minutes or till done. Cut slice from top of each. Scoop out inside and cube. Toss with ham and next 5 ingredients; spoon into potato shells. Bake at 425° for 15 minutes. Sprinkle American cheese atop. Heat 1 to 2 minutes more or till cheese melts. Serves 4.

BEEF RAREBIT

    1 pound ground beef
    ½ cup chopped onion
    ¼ cup chopped green pepper
    ¾ cup beer
        Dash cayenne
    12 ounces sharp process American
        cheese, shredded (3 cups)
    6 English muffins, split and
        toasted

Brown meat with vegetables; drain off fat. Add beer and cayenne. Stir in cheese; heat till melted. Serve over muffins. Serves 6.

Dazzle guests with a new version of the →
familiar meat and potato team. Make it a two-in-one entree with puffy Ham-Stuffed Potatoes laced with cheese.

GOURMET-SAUCED STEAK

½ cup light cream
¼ cup quick-cooking rolled oats
¼ cup chopped onion
1 teaspoon salt
1½ pounds ground sirloin
½ cup chopped fresh mushrooms
¼ cup finely chopped green onion
2 tablespoons butter or margarine
½ cup cold water
4 teaspoons cornstarch
1 cup red Burgundy
2 tablespoons snipped parsley
¾ teaspoon salt

Combine first 4 ingredients; add meat and mix well. Pat into a 6x5-inch rectangle 2 inches thick. Broil 4 inches from heat 10 to 12 minutes. Turn; broil 10 to 12 minutes more or to desired degree of doneness.

For sauce cook mushrooms and green onion in butter till tender. Blend cold water with cornstarch. Add to mushrooms with remaining ingredients. Cook and stir till thickened and bubbly. Pass with steak. Serves 6.

MOCK STROGANOFF

1 pound ground beef
¼ cup chopped onion
2 tablespoons all-purpose flour
1 teaspoon sugar
½ teaspoon dried basil leaves, crushed
⅛ teaspoon garlic powder
1 10½-ounce can condensed beef broth
1 6-ounce can tomato paste
1 3-ounce can sliced mushrooms, drained (½ cup)
1 cup dairy sour cream
Hot buttered noodles

In skillet cook meat and onion till meat is lightly browned. Combine flour, sugar, ½ teaspoon salt, basil, garlic powder, and ⅛ teaspoon pepper; sprinkle over meat. Stir in broth and tomato paste. Simmer, uncovered, 10 minutes, stirring occasionally. Stir in mushrooms and sour cream. Heat, but *do not boil*. Serve over noodles. Makes 6 servings.

VEAL BURGERS SCALLOPINI

Wine adds elegance to the sauce—

1 beaten egg
2 tablespoons milk
1 cup soft bread crumbs (about 1½ slices)
½ teaspoon salt
Dash pepper
1½ pounds ground veal
¼ cup all-purpose flour
¼ cup shortening
1 8-ounce can tomato sauce
1 3-ounce can (⅔ cup) chopped mushrooms, undrained
¼ cup sauterne
1 tablespoon finely snipped parsley
¼ teaspoon dried oregano leaves, crushed
Grated Parmesan cheese

Combine first 5 ingredients. Add veal; mix well. Shape into 6 patties; coat with flour. In skillet brown patties in hot shortening; drain off fat. Combine tomato sauce, mushrooms, wine, parsley, and oregano; pour over meat. Cover; simmer 20 to 25 minutes. To serve, sprinkle with Parmesan cheese. Serves 6.

HAMBURGER STROGANOFF

An economy version of the classic Stroganoff—

1 pound ground beef
3 slices bacon, diced
½ cup chopped onion
½ teaspoon salt
¼ teaspoon paprika
1 10½-ounce can condensed cream of mushroom soup
1 cup dairy sour cream
Hot buttered noodles

In skillet brown ground beef with bacon. Add onion; cook until tender but not brown. Drain off excess fat. Add salt, paprika, and dash pepper; stir in cream of mushroom soup. Cook slowly, uncovered, 20 minutes, stirring frequently. Stir in sour cream. Heat, but *do not boil*. Serve meat sauce over hot buttered noodles. Makes 4 to 6 servings.

SNAPPY BURGERS

Complement sweet-sour burgers with gingersnaps—

- 1 beaten egg
- 1 8-ounce can tomato sauce
- ⅓ cup crushed gingersnaps
  (6 gingersnaps)
- ⅓ cup finely chopped onion
- ¼ cup raisins
- 1½ pounds ground beef
  Shortening
- 2 tablespoons brown sugar
- 1 tablespoon vinegar
- 1 teaspoon prepared mustard
  Dash pepper

Combine egg, ¼ *cup* of the tomato sauce, gingersnaps, onion, raisins, and ¾ teaspoon salt. Add beef; mix well. Shape into 6 patties. In skillet brown patties in hot shortening. Pour off fat. Blend remaining tomato sauce with rest of ingredients; pour over patties. Cover; simmer 20 minutes spooning sauce over occasionally. Makes 6 servings.

SWEDISH MEAT BURGERS

- 1 beaten egg
- ½ cup dairy sour cream
- 1 cup soft bread crumbs
  (about 1½ slices)
- ½ cup finely chopped onion
- ½ teaspoon dry mustard
- ½ teaspoon ground mace
- 1 pound ground beef
- ½ pound ground pork
- ½ cup dairy sour cream
- ½ teaspoon onion salt
- 8 hamburger buns, split and
  toasted
  Shredded lettuce

Combine first 6 ingredients and 1 teaspoon salt. Add beef and pork; mix well. Shape into 8 patties. Brown slowly in skillet. Cover; continue cooking over low heat 15 minutes.

Meanwhile, blend remaining ½ cup sour cream with onion salt. To serve, place patties on toasted bun halves; spread with sour cream mixture. Top with shredded lettuce; cover with tops of buns. Makes 8 servings.

BEEF A LA WINE SAUCE

Colorful sauce teams wine with orange marmalade—

- 1 pound ground beef
- ½ cup Rosé wine
- 1½ teaspoons cornstarch
- 1 tablespoon lemon juice
- ¼ cup orange marmalade

Form meat into 4 patties about ¾ inch thick. Sprinkle with salt. Broil 3 to 4 inches from heat for 6 minutes. Turn; broil 4 minutes longer or to desired degree of doneness.

Meanwhile, in small saucepan blend wine with cornstarch. Stir in lemon juice and marmalade. Cook, stirring constantly, till mixture thickens and bubbles. To serve, garnish patties with orange slices, if desired. Spoon wine sauce atop. Makes 4 servings.

COMPANY MEATBALLS

A jiffy entree for last-minute guests—

- 2 beaten eggs
- ¼ cup milk
- ½ cup coarsely crushed saltine
  cracker crumbs (11 crackers)
- 1 teaspoon salt
  Dash ground thyme *or* ground
  oregano
- 1½ pounds ground beef
- 2 tablespoons shortening
- 1 beef bouillon cube
- 1 cup dairy sour cream
- 1 tablespoon all-purpose flour
- 1 6-ounce can sliced mushrooms,
  drained (1 cup)

Combine first 5 ingredients and dash pepper. Add beef; mix well. Shape into 30 balls. Brown slowly in hot shortening 15 to 20 minutes. Drain off fat. Dissolve bouillon cube in 1 cup boiling water; pour over balls. Cook, covered, over low heat 30 minutes. Remove meatballs, reserving pan juices.

In bowl blend sour cream with flour. Stir in ½ cup reserved pan juices; discard remaining pan juices. Return sauce to skillet. Add mushrooms and meatballs; stir to coat. Heat *just to boiling*. Makes 6 to 8 servings.

PLANKED MEAT LOAF

As pictured opposite chapter introduction—

    2 beaten eggs
    1 6-ounce can evaporated milk
    ½ cup finely crushed saltine
         cracker crumbs (14 crackers)
    2 tablespoons finely chopped onion
    ¼ teaspoon dried marjoram leaves,
         crushed
    1½ pounds ground beef
       Packaged instant mashed potatoes
         (enough for 8 servings)
    2 tablespoons sliced green onion
       Grated Parmesan cheese
    3 large tomatoes, halved crosswise
       Italian salad dressing

Combine first 5 ingredients and ¾ teaspoon salt. Add meat; mix well. Pat into 8½x4½x 2½-inch loaf dish. Bake at 350° for 1¼ hours. Remove from oven; let stand a few minutes. Remove from dish; place on seasoned plank or baking sheet. Prepare potatoes following package directions. Add green onion. "Frost" loaf with potatoes. Sprinkle with cheese.

Brush cut surfaces of tomatoes with Italian salad dressing; sprinkle with additional Parmesan. Arrange on plank with loaf. Broil 3 inches from heat for 5 minutes. Serves 6.

CHEESY HAM ROLL

    1 beaten egg
    ⅓ cup milk
    ½ cup soft bread crumbs
    1 tablespoon prepared mustard
    1 pound ground fully-cooked ham
    ½ pound ground pork
    4 slices process Swiss cheese
         (4 ounces)
    3 tablespoons snipped parsley

Combine first 4 ingredients. Add ham and pork; mix well. On waxed paper pat mixture into 14x7-inch rectangle. Arrange cheese atop meat; sprinkle with parsley. Roll jelly-roll fashion beginning with narrow side (see page 122). Press to seal ends and side seam. Place roll, seam side down, in 11x7x1½-inch baking pan. Bake at 350° for 45 minutes. Serves 6.

WILD RICE AND BEEF LOAF

    ½ 6-ounce package (⅓ cup)
         long-grain and wild rice mix
    ¼ cup chopped onion
    1 tablespoon butter or margarine
    1 3-ounce can chopped mushrooms
    1 beaten egg
    1 teaspoon Worcestershire sauce
    2 beaten eggs
    2 tablespoons fine dry bread
         crumbs
    2 pounds ground beef

Using 2 tablespoons of seasoning in rice mix package, cook rice following label directions. Cook onion in butter till tender. Drain mushrooms; reserve liquid. Mix 1 egg, rice, mushrooms, onion, and Worcestershire sauce; set aside.

Mix 2 eggs, reserved mushroom liquid, crumbs, and 1½ teaspoons salt. Add meat; mix well. Pat ⅓ of the meat into bottom of 9x5x3-inch baking dish. Top with rice mixture leaving ½-inch border on all sides. On waxed paper pat remaining meat to 11x7-inch rectangle. Invert over rice; discard paper. Press meat layers together at edges. Bake at 350° for 1¼ hours. Makes 8 servings.

COMPANY MEAT LOAF

Crunchy stuffing bakes atop meat loaf—

    ½ cup dairy sour cream
    2 tablespoons chopped green pepper
    1 pound ground beef
    ½ cup chopped onion
    ½ cup chopped celery
    2 tablespoons butter or margarine
    3 cups soft bread cubes (4 slices
         cut in ¼-inch cubes)
    1 beaten egg

Combine sour cream, green pepper, and ½ teaspoon salt. Add meat; mix well. Set aside. Cook onion and celery in butter till tender. Toss with bread, 1 tablespoon water, and ¼ teaspoon salt; stir in egg. Mix ⅓ *cup* bread mixture with meat. Shape into 5½x4-inch loaf on shallow baking pan. Bake at 350° for 45 minutes. Top with remaining bread mixture. Bake 30 minutes longer. Serves 4 or 5.

DILLY MEAT LOAF

Combine 2 beaten eggs; one 6-ounce can evaporated milk; ½ cup fine dry bread crumbs; ½ cup chopped onion; 1½ teaspoons dried dillweed; 1 teaspoon salt; ½ teaspoon Worcestershire sauce; and 1 small clove garlic, crushed. Add 2 pounds ground beef; mix well. Shape into loaf in 13x9x2-inch baking dish. Bake at 350° for 1¼ hours.

Mix ½ cup chili sauce and ½ teaspoon Worcestershire sauce. Spoon over loaf. Bake 15 minutes longer. Makes 8 servings.

LAMB-STUFFED ARTICHOKES

```
4 whole fresh artichokes
1 pound ground lamb
¾ cup chopped onion
2 tablespoons salad oil
½ cup fine dry bread crumbs
¼ cup snipped parsley
2 beaten eggs
¼ teaspoon ground nutmeg
¼ teaspoon pepper
  Sauterne Sauce
```

Wash artichokes; cut off stem close to base. Cook in boiling salted water 25 to 30 minutes or till stalk can be pierced easily and leaf pulled out readily. Drain upside down. Cut off top third of leaves with kitchen shears; remove center leaves and chokes.

Brown lamb and onion in hot oil; drain. Add crumbs, next 4 ingredients, and ½ teaspoon salt; mix well. Spread artichoke leaves slightly; fill centers with meat mixture. Place in 9x9x2-inch baking dish. Pour hot water around artichokes, 1 inch deep. Bake, uncovered, at 375° for 35 minutes.

Serve with *Sauterne Sauce:* Combine ¼ cup sauterne with 1 tablespoon instant minced onion; let stand 10 minutes. Add ¾ cup mayonnaise, 2 tablespoons snipped parsley, and 1 tablespoon lemon juice; mix well. Cook and stir till hot; *do not boil*. Serves 4.

Drizzle velvety Sauterne Sauce atop Lamb-Stuffed Artichokes for a sophisticated entree guaranteed to bring compliments from appreciative guests.

TRIPLE MEAT ROLL

Combine 3 cups dry bread cubes, ¼ cup raisins, ¼ cup chopped celery, 2 tablespoons chopped onion, ½ teaspoon ground sage, ¼ teaspoon salt, and dash pepper. Toss together with ½ cup beef broth *or* water; set aside.

Combine ½ pound ground beef, ½ pound ground veal, and ½ pound ground pork. Add 1 beaten egg, ¼ cup milk, 1 teaspoon salt, and dash pepper; mix well. On waxed paper pat meat mixture into 12x6-inch rectangle ½ inch thick. Spread with bread mixture; roll jelly-roll fashion beginning with long side (see page 122). Seal ends and side seam.

Place roll, seam side down, in 15½x10½x 1-inch baking pan. Place 8 slices bacon atop loaf. Bake at 350° for 1 hour. Serves 6 to 8.

Cooking for a Crowd

QUANTITY COOKING TIPS

The key to cooking for a large group of people is to keep the meal simple and uncomplicated. Casseroles and one-dish items are good choices. Keep them warm over a candle warmer or electric hot tray. Serve a salad, maybe a bread, a dessert, and a beverage with the casserole. With meat loaf, baked potatoes are a natural along with a colorful vegetable. Crisp crackers and relishes accompany chili, while potato chips team with barbecued sandwiches. Serve salads and desserts that can be made ahead of time.

Now that the menu is all set, plan how the meal is to be served. A hint—buffet service is easier on the hostess and tables are easier on the guests. So, set tables around the room and put the flatware, napkins, and coffee cups at place settings. Guests need only serve themselves main dish and salad.

BEEF AND CORN SUPPER

In Dutch oven cook 4 pounds ground beef, 2 cups chopped green pepper, and 1 cup chopped onion till vegetables are tender. Drain. Add three 16-ounce cans whole kernel corn, drained. In large bowl blend together four 10½-ounce cans condensed cream of chicken soup, four 10½-ounce cans condensed cream of mushroom soup, and 1 cup milk. Add to cooked meat mixture.

Cook one 7-ounce package macaroni according to package directions; drain. Divide between *two* 13x9x2-inch baking dishes. Pour half the meat mixture over each; mix.

Combine 1 cup fine dry bread crumbs and ¼ cup melted butter. Sprinkle half atop each casserole. Bake, uncovered, at 375° for 40 minutes or till heated through. Using 8 ounces sharp process American cheese, shredded (2 cups), sprinkle half over each casserole. Bake 4 to 5 minutes till cheese melts. Serves 24.

HAMBURGER-NOODLE BAKE

4 pounds ground beef
3 cups chopped onion
16 ounces medium noodles, cooked and drained
16 ounces sharp process American cheese, shredded (4 cups)
3 10¾-ounce cans condensed tomato soup
¾ cup chopped green pepper
½ cup chili sauce
¼ cup chopped canned pimiento
3 cups soft bread crumbs
6 tablespoons butter, melted

Divide beef and onion between 2 large skillets. Brown meat. Drain off fat. Combine meat and onion with noodles, cheese, soup, 3 cups water, green pepper, chili sauce, pimiento, 1½ teaspoons salt, and dash pepper. Mix. Turn into *two* 13x9x2-inch baking dishes. Combine crumbs and butter. Sprinkle atop casseroles. Bake, uncovered, at 350° for 40 to 45 minutes or till hot. Trim with green pepper rings, if desired. Serves 25 to 30.

HERBED MEAT LOAF

Combine 3 beaten eggs; 1½ cups milk; ⅓ cup catsup; 1 cup fine dry bread crumbs; ⅓ cup chopped onion; 3 tablespoons snipped parsley; 2 cloves garlic, minced; 1½ teaspoons salt; ¾ teaspoon *each* dried marjoram leaves, crushed, and dried oregano leaves, crushed; and ⅛ teaspoon pepper. Add 6 pounds ground beef; mix well. Shape into 3 loaves 7½x4-inches; square off ends. Place crosswise in 15½x10½x1-inch baking pan. Bake at 350° for 1¼ hours. Serves 24.

For that next church supper or family→ get-together, serve Hamburger-Noodle Bake. Serve it buffet style and pair with a refreshing molded fruit salad.

CHILI CON CARNE

        4 pounds ground beef
        4 large onions, chopped (4 cups)
        2 cups chopped green pepper
        4 16-ounce cans kidney beans,
             drained
        2 28-ounce cans tomatoes, cut up
        2 15-ounce cans tomato sauce
     1½ to 2 tablespoons chili powder
        ½ teaspoon paprika
        3 bay leaves, finely crushed

Season beef with 1 tablespoon salt. Brown meat in large kettle. Add onion and green pepper. Cook till tender. Add remaining ingredients. Cover; simmer 2 hours, stirring occasionally. Add water if needed for desired consistency. Makes 25 (about 1 cup) servings.

Present Chili Con Carne in a large bowl for buffet service and let guests help themselves. Accompany with crisp pickles.

MEXICAN-STYLE CASSEROLE

        5 pounds ground beef
        4 medium onions, chopped (2 cups)
        1 cup chopped green pepper
        1 tablespoon chili powder
        2 teaspoons dried oregano
             leaves, crushed
        2 teaspoons salt
        3 10½-ounce cans tomato puree
        2 28-ounce cans tomatoes, cut up
        2 16-ounce cans red kidney beans,
             drained
        5 cups crushed corn chips (about
             6 ounces)
        8 ounces process American cheese,
             shredded (2 cups)

Divide beef, onion, and green pepper between 2 large skillets. Cook till meat is browned and vegetables are tender; drain off excess fat. Divide next 6 ingredients and *4 cups* of the chips between the 2 skillets; mix. Simmer, uncovered, for 5 minutes. Turn into *two* 13x9x2-inch baking dishes. Bake, uncovered, at 350° for 35 minutes or till hot. Sprinkle remaining corn chips and cheese atop casseroles. Bake 5 minutes longer. Makes 24 servings.

SAUSAGE IN SPANISH RICE

        4 pounds bulk pork sausage
        4 medium onions, chopped (2 cups)
        2 cups chopped celery
        2 28-ounce cans tomatoes, cut up
     2½ cups uncooked long-grain rice
        5 cups water
        1 cup chili sauce
        8 ounces sharp process American
             cheese, shredded (2 cups)

Divide sausage between 2 large skillets. Brown sausage, breaking up with fork. Drain off fat. Add half the onion and celery to each skillet; cook till crisp-tender. Divide remaining ingredients except cheese between the 2 skillets; mix. Simmer, covered, for 10 minutes. Turn into *two* 13x9x2-inch baking dishes. Cover; bake at 350° for 25 to 30 minutes or till rice is done. Uncover; sprinkle each casserole with half the cheese. Return to oven to melt cheese. Makes 24 servings.

HAM AND MUSTARD SAUCE

Combine 3 beaten eggs; 1½ cups milk; 2 cups fine dry bread crumbs; and 1 cup *each* chopped onion, chopped green pepper, and chopped celery. Add 4 pounds ground fully-cooked ham and 2 pounds ground beef; mix well. Shape into three 7½x4-inch loaves, squaring off ends. Place in 15½x10½x1-inch baking pan. Bake at 350° for 1¼ hours. Serve with Mustard Sauce.

Mustard Sauce: In medium saucepan combine ¾ cup brown sugar and 2 tablespoons all-purpose flour. Gradually blend in 1½ cups cold water. Add ⅓ cup vinegar, 3 beaten eggs, ¼ cup prepared mustard, and ¼ teaspoon salt. Beat till smooth with rotary beater. Cook and stir over medium-low heat about 8 minutes till mixture thickens and bubbles. Cook and stir sauce 1 minute longer. Serve over ham loaf. Makes 24 servings.

BARBECUE SANDWICHES

Divide in half 4 pounds ground beef, 2 cups chopped onion, 2 cups chopped celery, and 1 cup chopped green pepper. Cook one portion at a time in 6-quart Dutch oven till meat is browned and vegetables are tender. To all of the meat mixture add two 15-ounce cans tomato sauce, 1 tablespoon Worcestershire sauce, 2 teaspoons salt, 1 teaspoon paprika, and 1 teaspoon chili powder.

Simmer, covered, 20 to 25 minutes, stirring occasionally. Spoon about ⅓ cup meat mixture into each of 25 to 30 split and toasted hamburger buns. Serves 25 to 30.

BEEF AND BEANS

Divide 4 pounds ground beef and 2 teaspoons salt between 2 large skillets. Brown meat. Drain off excess fat. Combine all of the meat with six 31-ounce cans pork and beans in tomato sauce; two 16-ounce cans kidney beans, drained; two 14-ounce bottles catsup; 2 cups chopped onion; 1 cup brown sugar; and 2 tablespoons dry mustard.

Turn into *two* large (5- or 6-quart) roasting pans. Bake, uncovered, at 350° for 2 to 2½ hours, stirring frequently. Serves 30.

SPAGHETTI AND MEATBALLS

Combine 3 beaten eggs, 1 cup milk, 1½ cups quick-cooking rolled oats, ½ cup chopped onion, 1 teaspoon Worcestershire sauce, 2 teaspoons salt, and ¼ teaspoon pepper. Add 2 pounds ground beef and 1 pound ground pork. Mix well. Shape into 6 dozen small meatballs. Place in shallow baking pan and brown at 350° for 20 to 25 minutes.

For sauce, cook 1½ cups chopped onion in ⅓ cup shortening till tender but not brown. Add four 15-ounce cans tomato sauce; 2½ cups water; 1 clove garlic, crushed; 1 tablespoon dried parsley flakes; 1 tablespoon dried basil leaves, crushed; 1 tablespoon sugar; 1 teaspoon salt; 1 teaspoon dried oregano leaves, crushed; and ¼ teaspoon pepper. Simmer 1 to 1¼ hours or to desired thickness. Add meatballs to sauce.

Cook 3½ to 4 pounds spaghetti according to package directions; drain. Serve sauce and meatballs over spaghetti. Makes 24 servings.

BEEF AND MACARONI

4 pounds ground beef
1 cup chopped onion
2 teaspoons salt
6 15-ounce cans macaroni in cheese sauce
2 10½-ounce cans condensed cream of celery soup
½ cup milk
⅓ cup snipped parsley
⅓ cup diced canned pimiento
½ teaspoon dried thyme leaves, crushed
6 ounces sharp process American cheese, shredded (1½ cups)
1 cup crushed potato chips

Divide beef, onion, and salt between 2 large skillets. Cook till meat is browned; drain off excess fat. Combine all of the meat with macaroni in cheese sauce (cutting up any long pieces of macaroni), soup, milk, parsley, pimiento, and thyme; mix well. Turn into *two* 13x9x2-inch baking dishes. Bake, uncovered, at 350° for 35 minutes. Combine cheese and potato chips; sprinkle half over top of each casserole. Bake 5 minutes more. Serves 24.

FAVORITES WITH A FOREIGN INFLUENCE

For a change of pace, plan the menu around a foreign theme. Choose from the many recipes that are adapted to ground meat and readily available ingredients.

Note that all meatballs are not alike. They are as distinctive as the countries from which they originate. Try those from Italy, Germany, Sweden, Greece, and the Orient. You'll find them exciting, different, and delicious.

And from our south-of-the-border neighbors try an assortment of tantalizing Mexican recipes.

Experiment, too, with mix-and-match pizza crusts and toppings to suit preference and preparation time. One crust starts from scratch, the other from a hot roll mix.

Olives, mushrooms, and wine make Olive-Spaghetti Sauce an extra-special treat. It's sure to become a favorite.

LASAGNE

1 pound Italian sausage
1 16-ounce can tomatoes, cut up
2 6-ounce cans tomato paste
1 clove garlic, minced
1 tablespoon dried basil
   leaves, crushed
10 ounces lasagne noodles
2 beaten eggs
3 cups fresh Ricotta *or* cream-style
   cottage cheese
½ cup grated Parmesan *or* Romano
   cheese
2 tablespoons dried parsley flakes
½ teaspoon pepper
1 pound mozzarella cheese, sliced
   very thin

For meat sauce, brown meat slowly; drain off fat. Add next 4 ingredients and 1½ teaspoons salt. Simmer, uncovered, 30 minutes; stir occasionally. Meanwhile, cook noodles in boiling salted water till tender; drain. For Ricotta filling, blend eggs, 1 teaspoon salt, and remaining ingredients except mozzarella. To assemble, layer *half* the noodles in 13x9x2-inch baking dish. Spread with *half* the Ricotta filling, *half* the mozzarella, and *half* the meat sauce. Repeat. Bake at 375° for 30 minutes. Let stand 10 minutes. Serves 8 to 10.

SAUCY SPINACH PATTIES

In skillet cook 1 pound ground beef and 1 cup chopped onion till meat is browned and onion is tender. Drain off excess fat.

Add one 16-ounce can tomatoes, cut up; one 8-ounce can tomato sauce; one 3-ounce can chopped mushrooms, drained; 1 clove garlic, minced; 1 teaspoon sugar; ¾ teaspoon salt; ½ teaspoon dried rosemary leaves, crushed; and ¼ teaspoon pepper. Cover; simmer 1¼ hours, stirring occasionally. Serve over hot *Spinach Patties:* Cook one 10-ounce package frozen chopped spinach following package directions; drain. Mix with ½ cup chopped onion, ½ cup shredded sharp process American cheese, ¼ cup snipped parsley, 2 beaten eggs, 2 cups soft bread crumbs, and ¼ teaspoon salt. Form into 6 patties. Brown in 3 tablespoons butter. Serves 6.

OLIVE-SPAGHETTI SAUCE

As shown opposite chapter introduction—

1 pound ground beef
½ pound ground veal
¼ pound Italian sausage
1 28-ounce can tomatoes, cut up
2 6-ounce cans tomato paste
1½ cups red Burgundy
1 cup chopped onion
¾ cup chopped green pepper
2 cloves garlic, crushed
1 teaspoon sugar
½ teaspoon chili powder
1½ teaspoons Worcestershire sauce
3 bay leaves
1 6-ounce can sliced mushrooms,
   drained (1 cup)
½ cup sliced pimiento-stuffed
   green olives
20 ounces spaghetti, cooked and
   drained

In large Dutch oven brown meats; drain off fat. Stir in 1 cup water, 1 teaspoon salt, ⅛ teaspoon pepper, tomatoes, and next 9 ingredients. Bring to boil; simmer, uncovered, 2 hours, stirring occasionally. Remove bay leaves. Add mushrooms and olives; simmer 30 minutes. Serve over spaghetti. Pass Parmesan cheese, if desired. Serves 8 to 10.

IN THE ITALIAN STYLE

Get out the red checkered tablecloth and plan an Italian party. Spaghetti or Lasagne are good choices when company comes. They can be prepared well in advance, avoiding last minute preparation.

A good way to start the meal is with antipasto—cheese wedges, pepperoni slices, olives, and pickled peppers. Other foods to serve would be a crisp green salad and crusty bread. Then, choose a light dessert. How about spumoni?

To make the party special, serve wine with the meal. Good choices would be a red Chianti or red Burgundy.

When serving spaghetti, be kind to guests' clothing by providing paper bibs as cover-ups, and conversation pieces.

ITALIAN MEAT SAUCE

In Dutch oven combine 1 pound ground beef, 1 cup chopped onion, and 2 cloves garlic, minced; cook till meat is browned and onion is tender. Drain off excess fat. Add one 28-ounce can tomatoes, cut up; one 16-ounce can tomatoes, cut up; 2 cups water; one 6-ounce can tomato paste; ¼ cup snipped parsley; 1 tablespoon brown sugar; 1½ teaspoons dried oregano leaves, crushed; 1 teaspoon salt; ¼ teaspoon dried thyme leaves, crushed; and 1 bay leaf. Simmer, uncovered, 3 hours or till sauce is thick; stir occasionally. Remove bay leaf. Serve over hot cooked spaghetti. Pass shredded Parmesan cheese. Serves 6.

TOMATO-SAUCED POLENTA

    ½ pound ground beef
    2 tablespoons chopped onion
    ½ clove garlic, crushed
    1 16-ounce can tomatoes, cut up
    1 8-ounce can tomato sauce
    1 3-ounce can (⅔ cup) sliced
        mushrooms, undrained
    2 tablespoons snipped parsley
    ½ teaspoon dried oregano leaves,
        crushed
    ¼ teaspoon salt
    ¼ teaspoon dried thyme leaves,
        crushed
    1 small bay leaf
      Polenta

In large saucepan cook ground beef with onion and garlic till meat is brown. Drain off fat. Add ⅓ cup water and remaining ingredients except Polenta. Bring to boiling; reduce heat. Simmer, uncovered, for 1¼ hours or till thick. Stir occasionally. Remove bay leaf. Serve over squares of Polenta. Pass Parmesan cheese, if desired. Serves 6.

Polenta: In saucepan bring 2½ cups water to boiling. Combine 1½ cups yellow cornmeal, 1½ cups cold water, and 1½ teaspoons salt. Stir into boiling water. Cook and stir till thick. Cover; cook over very low heat about 45 minutes, stirring occasionally. Spread in 8x8x2-inch baking pan. Cool thoroughly. Cut into 6 pieces. Brown in ¼ cup butter till golden, about 5 to 6 minutes per side.

SPAGHETTI AND MEATBALLS

    ¾ cup chopped onion
    1 clove garlic, minced
    3 tablespoons salad oil
    2 16-ounce cans tomatoes, cut up
    2 6-ounce cans tomato paste
    1½ teaspoons salt
    1½ teaspoons dried oregano leaves,
        crushed
    1 teaspoon sugar
    ½ teaspoon pepper
    1 bay leaf
      Italian Meatballs (see below)
      Hot cooked spaghetti
      Parmesan cheese

Cook onion and garlic in salad oil till tender but not brown. Stir in tomatoes, tomato paste, 2 cups water, salt, oregano, sugar, pepper, and bay leaf. Simmer, uncovered, 30 minutes. Remove bay leaf. Add browned Italian meatballs. Loosely cover and simmer 30 minutes. Serve over hot cooked spaghetti. Pass Parmesan cheese. Makes 8 servings.

ITALIAN MEATBALLS

Another time serve an Americanized version without spaghetti and tomato sauce. Simmer meatballs in a mushroom sauce and spoon over noodles—

    4 slices bread
    ½ cup water
    2 beaten eggs
    ¼ cup grated Parmesan cheese
    2 tablespoons snipped parsley
    1 teaspoon salt
    ¼ teaspoon dried oregano leaves,
        crushed
    1 pound ground beef
    2 tablespoons salad oil
      Spaghetti Sauce (see above)

Soak bread in water 2 to 3 minutes. Add eggs, Parmesan, parsley, salt, oregano, and dash pepper; mix well. Add beef and mix thoroughly. Form mixture into 24 small balls. Brown in hot salad oil. Add meatballs to Spaghetti Sauce. Simmer loosely covered for 30 minutes as directed for Spaghetti and Meatballs (see above). Makes 8 servings.

HOMEMADE PIZZA CRUST

Soften 1 package active dry yeast in 1 cup *warm* water (110°). Beat in 1½ cups sifted all-purpose flour; mix in 1 tablespoon salad oil and 1 teaspoon salt. Stir in 2 cups flour. Knead till smooth and elastic, about 12 minutes (will be firm). Place in lightly greased bowl; turn greased side up. Cover. Let rise in warm place till more than double, 1½ to 2 hours. Punch down; cover and chill.

Cut dough in half. On lightly floured surface, roll each into 12-inch circle, about ⅛ inch thick. Place in two greased 12-inch pizza pans; crimp edges. Brush each circle with 1 tablespoon salad oil. Fill with desired topping. Bake at 425° for 20 to 25 minutes. Makes two 12-inch pizza crusts.

JIFFY PIZZA CRUST

Using 1 cup warm water (110°) and no egg, prepare one 13¾-ounce package hot roll mix according to package directions. *Do not let rise.* Cut in half. With oiled hands, pat each into 12-inch circle on greased baking sheet; crimp edges. Brush circle with about 1 tablespoon salad oil. Fill with desired topping. Bake at 450° about 20 minutes or till crusts are done. Makes two 12-inch pizza crusts.

ITALIAN PIZZA

    1 pound bulk pork sausage
 1½ teaspoons *each* dried oregano
       leaves and basil leaves, crushed
    1 15-ounce can tomato sauce
    2 12-inch pizza dough circles
    1 6-ounce can sliced mushrooms,
       drained (1 cup)
   ¼ cup sliced pitted ripe olives
    1 6-ounce package sliced mozzarella
       cheese, torn in pieces

In skillet slowly brown sausage, breaking up sausage as it cooks. Drain off excess fat. Stir in oregano and basil. Spread tomato sauce over pizza dough circles; top with sausage mixture, mushrooms, olives, and then cheese. Bake as for type of pizza dough used. Makes two 12-inch pizzas.

GROUND BEEF PIZZA

 1½ pounds ground beef
    1 small clove garlic, minced
    1 teaspoon dried oregano leaves,
       crushed
    2 8-ounce cans tomato sauce with
       mushrooms
    2 12-inch pizza dough circles
    1 small onion, sliced and
       separated into rings
    1 medium green pepper, cut into
       rings
    1 6-ounce package sliced mozzarella
       cheese, torn in pieces
   ¼ cup grated Parmesan cheese

In skillet brown beef; drain off excess fat. Add garlic and oregano. Spread tomato sauce over pizza dough circles; top with meat. Arrange onion and green pepper rings atop meat. Cover with mozzarella cheese, then sprinkle with Parmesan. Bake as for type of pizza dough used. Makes two 12-inch pizzas.

SHORT-CUT PIZZA

No one will ever guess that this pizza uses leftover meat loaf—

    1 package cheese pizza mix
       (for 1 pizza)
   ½ teaspoon dried oregano leaves,
       crushed
   ¼ teaspoon garlic powder
    2 cups crumbled leftover meat
       loaf
    1 3-ounce can sliced mushrooms,
       drained (½ cup)
    1 4-ounce package (1 cup)
       shredded pizza cheese

Prepare pizza dough following package directions. Roll or pat out to fit 12-inch pizza pan. Place in greased 12-inch pizza pan; crimp edges. Blend oregano and garlic powder with pizza sauce (from package mix); spread over pizza dough. Cover with crumbled meat loaf, mushrooms, then pizza cheese. Sprinkle atop grated cheese (from package mix). Bake at 425° about 20 minutes or till crust is done. Makes one 12-inch pizza.

MEXICAN MEAT PATTIES

Reserving the sauce, drain one 15-ounce can tamales in sauce. Mash tamales. Add 1 pound ground beef, 2 tablespoons milk, ½ teaspoon chili powder, ¼ teaspoon garlic salt, and ¼ teaspoon salt; mix well. Shape into 6 patties, ¾ inch thick. Broil 3 inches from heat 8 minutes. Turn; broil 6 to 8 minutes.

Meanwhile, cut 6 large tortillas into ¼-inch strips. Melt 2 tablespoons shortening in skillet. Add tortilla strips and cook quickly till soft and lightly browned. *Or* omit tortillas and use corn chips. Turn tortillas or corn chips into serving dish and top with meat patties. Heat reserved sauce from tamales and drizzle over patties. Makes 6 servings.

CHILIES RELLENOS

3 fresh long green hot peppers *or* canned peeled green chilies *or* small fresh green peppers
½ pound ground beef
¼ cup chopped onion
6 slices sharp process American cheese
6 eggs
3 tablespoons all-purpose flour
Fat for frying

To prepare fresh peppers, place on baking sheet in 450° oven for about 15 minutes or till skins form black blisters, giving a quarter turn once. (Peppers will be cooked.) Cool slightly. Peel and remove stems and seeds. Cut each pepper in half lengthwise.

Cook beef, onion, and ¼ teaspoon salt in skillet till lightly browned. Stuff each pepper half with about ¼ cup meat mixture. Top with cheese slice. Separate eggs. Beat whites till stiff, but not dry, peaks form. To yolks add flour and ¼ teaspoon salt. Beat till thick and lemon-colored. Fold into whites.

For each pepper, spoon about ⅓ cup of egg batter into ½-inch hot fat (375°) in skillet; spread batter into a circle. As batter begins to set, gently top each mound with a stuffed pepper. Cover with another ⅓ cup batter. Continue cooking till underside is browned, 2 to 3 minutes. Turn carefully; brown second side. Drain. Serve at once. Serves 6.

MEXICAN SURPRISES

An egg wedge hides in each meatball—

In skillet cook 2 tablespoons chopped onion and 1 clove garlic, crushed, in 1 tablespoon salad oil till tender but not brown. Blend in ¼ cup chili sauce and all but ½ *cup* of one 10½-ounce can condensed beef broth.

In mixing bowl combine 1 beaten egg, ½ cup milk, 1½ cups soft bread crumbs (about 2 slices), and 1 teaspoon salt. Add 1½ pounds ground beef; mix well. Cut each of 3 hard-cooked eggs into 6 wedges. Divide meat mixture into 18 portions. Wet hands; form one portion of meat around each egg wedge. Place meatballs in skillet with beef broth mixture. Bring to boiling; reduce heat and simmer, covered, 20 minutes, turning once. Remove meatballs to platter; reserve sauce.

Blend together ¼ cup all-purpose flour and reserved ½ cup beef broth. Stir into reserved sauce in skillet; cook and stir till bubbly. Pour over meatballs. Sprinkle with ⅓ cup chopped almonds, if desired. Makes 6 servings.

MEXICAN CASSEROLE

1½ pounds ground beef
1 cup chopped onion
1 16-ounce can tomatoes, cut up
1 8-ounce can tomato sauce
½ cup raisins
3 hard-cooked eggs, chopped
¾ teaspoon salt
¼ teaspoon Worcestershire sauce
Dash bottled hot pepper sauce
2 cups packaged biscuit mix
2 teaspoons yellow cornmeal

In skillet cook meat and onion till meat is browned. Drain off fat. Add tomatoes, tomato sauce, raisins, eggs, salt, Worcestershire, and bottled hot pepper sauce. Bring to boiling; boil, uncovered, 5 minutes.

Meanwhile, using 2 cups biscuit mix, prepare dumplings following directions on biscuit mix package. Turn boiling meat mixture into 12x7½x2-inch baking dish; top with dumplings. Sprinkle dumplings with cornmeal. Bake, uncovered, at 400° for 18 to 20 minutes, or till dumplings are done. Serves 8.

TAMALE PIE

In large skillet cook 1 pound ground beef, 1 cup chopped onion, and 1 cup chopped green pepper till meat is browned. Stir in two 8-ounce cans tomato sauce; one 12-ounce can whole kernel corn, drained; ½ cup pitted ripe olives, chopped; 1 clove garlic, minced; 1 tablespoon sugar; 1 teaspoon salt; 2 to 3 teaspoons chili powder; and dash pepper. Simmer, uncovered, 20 to 25 minutes or till thick. Add 6 ounces sharp process American cheese shredded (1½ cups); stir till melted. Turn into greased 9x9x2-inch baking dish.

Make Cornmeal Topper: Stir ¾ cup yellow cornmeal and ½ teaspoon salt into 2 cups cold water. Cook and stir till thick. Add 1 tablespoon butter; mix. Spoon over *boiling* meat. Bake at 375° about 40 minutes. Serves 6.

BEEF TACOS

1 pound ground beef
½ cup chopped onion
1 clove garlic, minced
½ teaspoon chili powder
12 tortillas (frozen or canned)
   Shortening
2 tomatoes, chopped and drained
3 cups finely shredded lettuce
8 ounces natural Cheddar cheese, shredded (2 cups)
   Canned Mexican hot sauce *or* canned enchilada sauce

In skillet cook beef, onion, and garlic till meat is browned. Drain. Add ½ teaspoon salt and chili powder. Set aside; keep warm.

In heavy skillet fry tortillas, one at a time, in ¼ inch hot shortening. When tortilla becomes limp, fold in half with tongs and hold edges apart while frying to allow for filling. Fry 1½ to 2 minutes or till crisp. Drain. Spoon about ¼ cup meat mixture into each. Top with tomato, lettuce, and cheese. Serve with hot sauce. Makes 6 servings.

◄─ Fill taco shells with a mildly seasoned meat mixture, then top with tomato, lettuce, and cheese. Hot sauce is poured over Beef Tacos to suit individual taste.

PUFFY TORTILLA BAKE

For Sauce: Cook ¾ cup chopped onion in 1 tablespoon salad oil till tender but not brown. Add one 16-ounce can tomatoes, cut up; one 8-ounce can tomato sauce; 1 clove garlic, minced; 1 to 1½ teaspoons finely chopped canned green chilies; 1½ teaspoons chili powder; 1 teaspoon sugar, and ½ teaspoon salt. Simmer, uncovered, 30 minutes.

For Filling: Cook ¾ pound ground beef and 1 small clove garlic, minced, in 1 tablespoon salad oil. Add ½ cup sliced green onion, 3 tablespoons chopped pitted ripe olives, 2 teaspoons chili powder, and ½ teaspoon salt; stir to blend ingredients.

Prepare Puffy Tortillas: Sift together ¾ cup sifted all-purpose flour, ¾ cup yellow cornmeal, and ¼ teaspoon salt. Add 1 beaten egg and 1¾ cups water. Beat smooth. Making 12 tortillas, pour 3 tablespoons batter at a time in hot greased 6-inch skillet; cook till browned on bottom and top is just set, 2 to 3 minutes. Loosen tortillas with spatula; flip out onto paper toweling to drain.

Shred 6 ounces sharp process American cheese (1½ cups). With browned side down, fill each tortilla with 2 to 3 tablespoons Filling and 1 tablespoon cheese; roll up.

Arrange 12 filled tortillas in 12x7½x2-inch baking dish. Pour cooked Sauce over; sprinkle with remaining cheese and ¼ cup pitted ripe olives, sliced lengthwise. Bake at 350° for 25 to 30 minutes. Makes 4 to 6 servings.

IN THE MEXICAN WAY

Looking for something different to serve guests at an evening get-together? Try a Mexican party and serve make-it-yourself Tacos. Each guest fills a crisp taco shell with desired ingredients, then pours on as much hot sauce as desired.

The appetizer problem is solved when Guacamole is served. It's a dip (salad) that's prepared from avocado and is perfectly paired with crisp tortilla chips.

And for a beverage, have Mexican chocolate on hand. It's good for those who don't imbibe in something potent. Serve in mugs with cinnamon stick stirrers to make the drink special.

SWEDISH MEATBALLS

Have ¾ pound ground beef, ½ pound ground veal, and ¼ pound ground pork ground together twice. Soak 1½ cups soft bread crumbs (about 2 slices) in 1 cup light cream about 5 minutes. Cook ½ cup chopped onion in 1 tablespoon butter till tender.

Combine 1 beaten egg, crumb mixture, onion, ¼ cup finely snipped parsley, 1¼ teaspoons salt, dash pepper, dash ground ginger, and dash ground nutmeg. Add meats. Beat 5 minutes at medium speed on electric mixer, or mix by hand until well combined. Form into 30 balls (mixture will be soft—for easier shaping, wet hands or chill mixture).

In skillet brown meatballs in 2 tablespoons butter. Remove from skillet; reserve drippings. For gravy melt 2 tablespoons butter in skillet with drippings. Stir in 2 tablespoons all-purpose flour. Add 1 beef bouillon cube dissolved in 1¼ cups boiling water and ½ teaspoon instant coffee powder. Cook and stir till gravy thickens and bubbles. Add meatballs. Cover. Cook slowly about 30 minutes; baste occasionally. Makes 6 to 8 servings.

GREEK MEATBALLS

    2 beaten eggs
    ¾ cup milk
    ¾ cup fine dry bread crumbs
    ½ cup finely chopped onion
    ¾ cup snipped parsley
    1 clove garlic, crushed
 1½ teaspoons salt
    ¼ teaspoon dried mint flakes,
        crushed
      Dash pepper
    2 pounds ground lamb *or*
        ground beef
    2 tablespoons shortening
    3 tablespoons lemon juice

Combine first 9 ingredients. Add meat; mix well. Form into 40 balls. In large skillet brown meatballs slowly in hot shortening, about 10 minutes. Cook over low heat till done, about 10 to 12 minutes. Remove meatballs to serving dish; reserve drippings. Pour lemon juice in skillet. Heat, scraping up drippings. Pour over meatballs. Makes 8 to 10 servings.

KÖNIGSBERGER KLOPS

    1 2-ounce can anchovy fillets
    5 slices dry bread
    1 cup milk
 1½ cups chopped onion
    2 tablespoons butter or margarine
            •   •   •
    2 beaten eggs
 1½ teaspoons salt
    ¼ teaspoon pepper
    1 pound ground beef
    ½ pound ground veal
    ½ pound ground pork
    ¾ cup sauterne
    ¾ cup water
    1 bay leaf
    4 whole cloves
    4 peppercorns
            •   •   •
    2 tablespoons all-purpose flour
    ¼ cup cold water
    1 lemon, very thinly sliced
    1 tablespoon capers
    ¼ teaspoon salt
      Hot cooked noodles
      Snipped parsley

To desalt anchovies, soak in cold water to cover about 20 minutes; drain well. Soak bread in milk. Cook onion in butter till tender but not brown. Combine eggs, anchovies, bread mixture, onion, 1½ teaspoons salt, and pepper. Add meats; mix well. Form into 24 large meatballs (klops).

In very large skillet combine wine, ¾ cup water, bay leaf, cloves, and peppercorns. Add meatballs. Cover; simmer 25 to 30 minutes. Remove meatballs and strain liquid. Return liquid to skillet. Blend flour and ¼ cup cold water till smooth. Stir into hot liquid; cook and stir till mixture thickens and bubbles. Add lemon slices, capers, and ¼ teaspoon salt. Cook 1 or 2 minutes longer. Arrange meatballs on platter of hot cooked noodles. Pour sauce over all. Garnish with snipped parsley. Makes 8 servings.

**Round-out a German dinner starring →
Königsberger Klops with sweet-sour red cabbage, rye bread, apple strudel, and a big mug of beer or piping hot coffee.**

GREEK MOUSSAKA

Peel 2 medium eggplants; cut into slices ½ inch thick. Sprinkle slices with a little salt and set aside.

Meat Layer: In skillet brown 1 pound ground beef with 1 cup chopped onion; drain. Add ¼ cup red Burgundy, ¼ cup water, 2 tablespoons snipped parsley, 1 tablespoon tomato paste, 1 teaspoon salt, and dash pepper. Simmer till liquid is nearly absorbed. Cool. Stir in ⅓ cup soft bread crumbs (½ slice), 2 beaten eggs, ¼ cup shredded sharp process American cheese, and dash ground cinnamon.

Sauce: In saucepan melt 3 tablespoons butter. Stir in 3 tablespoons all-purpose flour. Add 1½ cups milk; cook and stir till bubbly. Add ½ teaspoon salt, dash pepper, and dash ground nutmeg. Add small amount of sauce to 1 beaten egg; return to hot mixture. Cook and stir over low heat 2 minutes.

Brown eggplant slices on both sides in a little hot salad oil. Sprinkle bottom of 12x7½x 2-inch baking dish with ⅓ cup soft bread crumbs (½ slice). Cover with *half* of the eggplant slices. Spoon on all of meat mixture. Arrange remaining eggplant over meat mixture. Pour milk-egg sauce over all. Top with ¼ cup shredded sharp process American cheese. Bake at 350° for about 45 minutes. Serve hot. Makes 6 to 8 servings.

GOULASH

  1½ cups thinly sliced onion
    2 tablespoons butter
  1½ pounds ground beef
  1½ teaspoons paprika
    1 beef bouillon cube
    2 medium raw potatoes, peeled
      and cubed
   ¼ cup chili sauce
   ½ cup dairy sour cream

In 3-quart saucepan cook onion in butter till tender but not brown. Remove from saucepan. In same saucepan brown beef. Add onion, paprika, and 1 teaspoon salt. Dissolve bouillon cube in 1 cup boiling water. Stir into meat with potatoes and chili sauce. Cover; simmer 15 to 20 minutes. Stir in sour cream; heat, *but do not boil*. Makes 6 servings.

LAMB CURRY

Use ground lamb for a variation of Indian curry—

    1 pound ground lamb
    1 cup chopped onion
    1 clove garlic, minced
    2 tablespoons butter or margarine
    2 tomatoes, peeled and chopped
   ¼ cup water
    1 to 1½ teaspoons curry powder
   ¾ teaspoon salt
   ½ teaspoon ground ginger
    1 tablespoon all-purpose flour
    3 cups hot cooked rice
      Curry condiments

In skillet cook lamb, onion, and garlic in butter, breaking up lamb as it cooks. Cook till onion is tender and meat is browned. Drain off excess fat. Add tomatoes, ¼ cup water, curry powder, salt, and ginger. Cover and simmer 30 minutes, stirring occasionally. Blend flour and ¼ cup cold water; add to meat mixture. Cook and stir till bubbly. Serve over hot cooked rice. Pass curry condiments of sliced green onion, shredded coconut, raisins, and peanuts. Serves 6.

KIMA

Spark the menu with a Pakistani favorite—

    1 pound ground beef
    1 cup chopped onion
    1 clove garlic, minced
    2 tomatoes, peeled and cubed
    2 raw potatoes, peeled and cubed
    1 10-ounce package frozen peas,
      broken apart
    2 teaspoons curry powder
  1½ teaspoons salt
      Dash pepper
      Flaked coconut
      Hot cooked rice

In skillet cook beef, onion, and garlic till meat is browned. Pour off fat. Stir in remaining ingredients except coconut and rice. Cover; simmer for 20 to 25 minutes or till vegetables are tender. Sprinkle with coconut. Serve with hot cooked rice. Makes 6 servings.

AMERICAN CHOP SUEY

In skillet cook 1 pound ground pork till lightly browned. Drain off excess fat. Add one 16-ounce can bean sprouts, drained; 1 cup bias-cut celery; ½ cup coarsely chopped onion; one 5-ounce can water chestnuts, drained and sliced; one 3-ounce can sliced mushrooms, drained (½ cup); and all but ¼ *cup* of one 10½-ounce can condensed beef broth. Bring mixture to boiling; reduce heat. Simmer, covered, 15 minutes.

Blend 2 tablespoons soy sauce with 2 tablespoons cornstarch and the reserved ¼ cup beef broth. Stir into meat-vegetable mixture. Cook and stir till thickened and bubbly. Serve over hot cooked rice. Sprinkle ¼ cup toasted slivered almonds atop. Pass additional soy sauce. Makes 6 servings.

BEEF AND EGG FOO YONG

1 tablespoon cornstarch
2 teaspoons sugar
1 cup water
2 tablespoons soy sauce
1 teaspoon vinegar

• • •

½ pound ground beef
6 well-beaten eggs
½ 16-ounce can bean sprouts, drained (1 cup)
¼ cup finely chopped onion
¼ cup finely chopped celery
½ teaspoon salt
1 tablespoon shortening
Hot cooked rice

In small saucepan combine cornstarch and sugar. Gradually blend in water, soy sauce, and vinegar. Cook and stir till thickened and bubbly. Cook 1 minute more. Keep warm.

Cook beef in skillet until lightly browned. Drain off fat. Add meat to beaten eggs with bean sprouts, onion, celery, and salt.

Heat shortening on griddle. Using ¼ cup meat-egg mixture for each patty, pour on griddle. Shape patties with a pancake turner by pushing egg back into the patties. When set and brown on one side, turn to brown other side. Serve with hot cooked rice. Pour sauce over patties and rice. Serves 4 or 5.

ORIENTAL PORK AND SHRIMP

Dandy as a hot hors d'oeuvre also—

2 beaten eggs
½ pound ground pork
1 7-ounce package (1 cup) frozen cleaned shelled shrimp, thawed and finely chopped
1 5-ounce can water chestnuts, drained and chopped
2 tablespoons chopped green onion
1 teaspoon soy sauce
½ teaspoon sugar
½ cup fine dry bread crumbs
Fat for frying
Sweet-Sour Sauce

Combine first 7 ingredients and ¼ teaspoon salt; mix well. Shape into 36 balls. Roll in bread crumbs. Fry in deep hot fat (360°) until brown, for 1½ to 2 minutes.

Serve with *Sweet-Sour Sauce:* In saucepan combine ¾ cup water, ¼ cup sugar, 2 tablespoons vinegar, 1 tablespoon soy sauce, and ¼ teaspoon salt. Heat to boiling. Blend together 1 tablespoon cornstarch and 1 tablespoon cold water. Slowly stir into boiling mixture. Cook and stir till bubbly. Serves 6.

POLISH MEAT TARTS

Appetizer favorite—like miniature Cornish pasty—

In skillet brown ½ pound ground beef with ¼ cup chopped onion. Drain. Add 1 hardcooked egg, chopped; ¼ teaspoon salt; and dash pepper. Combine 1 teaspoon all-purpose flour and ¼ cup cold water; stir into meat mixture. Cook and stir till bubbly; set aside.

Combine 1 cup sifted all-purpose flour and ¾ teaspoon salt. Cut in ¼ cup butter. Stir in ½ cup dairy sour cream. Chill. Roll to 15x12-inch rectangle. Cut 1 tablespoon chilled butter in small pieces; scatter over dough. Fold dough over in thirds. Roll out again to same size rectangle; fold in thirds. Chill. Roll to 15x12-inch rectangle. Cut in 3-inch rounds. Spoon meat mixture on *half* of the rounds; top with remaining rounds. Seal edges together firmly with tines of fork. Bake at 375° for 25 minutes. Makes 12 to 14 meat tarts.

MEALS IN A HURRY

Running short on time? Check this section for quick and easy recipes. Then stock the pantry shelves with basic canned foods and convenience items for hurry-up meals.

Hamburgers and meal-in-a-dish soups are a boon to busy homemakers—perfect for lunch or supper. Discover the countless variety of ways to prepare hamburgers, selecting a different burger recipe each time. Or try a new sandwich idea when meals must be served on short notice. Fix hefty sandwiches on French bread for hungry youngsters, or more sophisticated sandwiches for grown-ups.

The freezer can also be a lifesaver. Just prepare the Basic Ground Beef mixture and have it on hand as the start for quick and easy sandwiches, skillets, and casseroles.

A trio of hamburgers for eating enjoyment—Iowa Corn Burgers, German Burgers, and Orange-Topped Burgers.

Quick-fix Recipes

QUICK CHINESE COMBO

1 pound ground beef
1 cup bias-cut celery slices
1 10½-ounce can condensed cream
   of mushroom soup
⅔ cup water
1 8-ounce can cut green beans,
   drained
1 5-ounce can water chestnuts,
   drained and sliced
1 tablespoon soy sauce
1 16-ounce can tomatoes, drained
   and cut up *or* 2 medium fresh
   tomatoes, cut in wedges
   Chinese noodles

In skillet cook beef with celery till meat is browned and celery is crisp-tender. Drain off fat. Add soup and next 4 ingredients; simmer 5 minutes, stirring occasionally. Add tomatoes; heat through. Serve over Chinese noodles. Pass soy sauce, if desired. Serves 4.

HAM PINWHEELS

2 cups ground fully-cooked ham
2 tablespoons brown sugar
2 teaspoons prepared mustard
1 teaspoon Worcestershire sauce
¼ cup butter or margarine, melted
1 package refrigerated biscuits
   (10 biscuits)
1 10¾-ounce can condensed
   Cheddar cheese soup
⅛ cup milk

Combine first 5 ingredients. Separate biscuits; arrange side by side, in two rows of 5 biscuits each. Pat biscuits together to form a 12x6-inch rectangle about ¼ inch thick. Spread ham mixture on biscuits. Roll up jelly-roll fashion starting with long side. Cut into 8 rolls. Place in shallow baking pan, cut side up. Bake at 400° for 12 to 15 minutes. Meanwhile, in saucepan heat soup with milk. Serve over pinwheels. Makes 4 servings.

FRENCH FRY-BURGER PIE

1 pound ground beef
1 cup chopped celery
¾ cup chopped onion
1 10¾-ounce can condensed
   tomato soup
⅛ cup catsup
1 9-ounce package frozen French-
   fried potatoes

In skillet cook meat, celery, and onion till meat is browned and vegetables are tender. Drain off fat. Stir in soup, catsup, ¾ teaspoon salt, and dash pepper. Turn into 8x8x2-inch baking dish. Arrange potatoes over top. Bake at 425° for 25 minutes. Serves 4 to 6.

SAUSAGE-POTATO PIZZA

In skillet break up ½ pound bulk pork sausage; cook slowly till lightly browned. Drain off fat. Arrange one 16-ounce package frozen French-fried potatoes in a layer in bottom of 12x7½x2-inch baking dish. Top with one 6-ounce package sliced mozzarella cheese (4 slices); spread one 8-ounce can pizza sauce over cheese. Sprinkle sausage over sauce. Bake at 450° for 25 to 30 minutes. Cut into squares. Serve immediately. Serves 4 to 6.

HAM WITH ORANGE RICE

3 tablespoons chopped green pepper
2 tablespoons chopped onion
2 tablespoons butter or margarine
2 tablespoons brown sugar
2 cups coarsely ground or finely
   chopped fully-cooked ham
2 cups cooked rice
⅛ cup orange juice
1 teaspoon grated orange peel

Cook green pepper and onion in butter till tender. Stir in brown sugar. Add remaining ingredients; mix well. Heat through. Serves 4.

BEEF-MACARONI COMBO

    2 beaten eggs
    ½ cup catsup
    ⅓ cup milk
    1 tablespoon instant minced onion
    1 pound ground beef
    1 14-ounce package macaroni and
        cheese deluxe dinner
    ⅓ cup chopped green pepper
    2 teaspoons prepared mustard
    ½ cup packaged garlic croutons

Combine first 4 ingredients and 1 teaspoon salt. Add beef and mix well. Cook macaroni following package directions; drain. Stir in green pepper, mustard, and *one-half* the cheese sauce mix from macaroni package. Spread in greased 12x7½x2-inch baking dish. Top with meat mixture. Dot with remaining sauce mix; sprinkle with croutons. Bake, uncovered, at 350° for 35 to 40 minutes. Serves 6 to 8.

Creamy macaroni and cheese nestles under meat loaf in Beef-Macaroni Combo for a speedy main dish using a mix.

SAUSAGE-MUFFIN BAKE

    1 pound bulk pork sausage
    1 16-ounce can whole cranberry
        sauce
    1 medium orange, peeled and cut up
    1 8-ounce package corn muffin mix

Brown sausage, breaking up into small pieces; drain. Spread meat in 8x8x2-inch baking dish. Top with cranberry, then with orange. Prepare muffin mix following package directions. Pour over fruit; spread to edges. Bake at 375° for 35 to 40 minutes. Serves 6.

SPEEDY CORN BREAD PIE

    2 15-ounce cans barbecue sauce
        and beef
    1 8-ounce can kidney beans,
        drained
    1 8-ounce package corn muffin mix

Combine first 2 ingredients; bring to boiling. Pour into 1½-quart casserole. Prepare corn muffin mix following package directions. Spread atop *hot* meat mixture. Bake at 400° for 20 to 25 minutes. Makes 6 servings.

QUICKY TURNOVERS

    1 pound ground beef
    ¼ cup chopped onion
    2 teaspoons dried parsley flakes
    ½ teaspoon salt
      Dash pepper
    2 packages refrigerated buttermilk
        biscuits (20 biscuits)
    ⅓ cup grated Parmesan cheese
    1 10½-ounce can condensed cream
        of mushroom soup
    ⅓ cup milk

In skillet brown meat with onion. Drain off excess fat. Add parsley, salt, and pepper; mix well. On lightly floured surface roll 2 of the packaged biscuits, overlapping edges slightly, into a 6x5-inch oval. Spoon about ¼ cup meat mixture on half of the oval; sprinkle with 1½ teaspoons Parmesan cheese.

Fold biscuit over; pinch edges together to seal. Place on ungreased baking sheet; prick top with fork. Repeat with remaining biscuits. Bake at 425° for 8 to 10 minutes or till browned. Blend soup with milk; heat and stir. Serve over turnovers. Makes 10 servings.

SWEET-SOUR MEATBALLS

Drain one 8¾-ounce can pineapple tidbits, reserving syrup. In medium saucepan combine ¼ cup brown sugar with 2 tablespoons cornstarch. Blend in ½ cup cold water; add reserved syrup, ¼ cup cider vinegar, and 1 teaspoon soy sauce. Cook, stirring constantly, till mixture thickens and bubbles.

Carefully stir in one 16-ounce can meatballs in gravy; one 5-ounce can water chestnuts, drained and thinly sliced; 1 green pepper, cut in strips; and drained pineapple. Heat mixture to boiling. Serve with mounds of fluffy hot cooked rice. Trim with tomato wedges, if desired. Makes 4 servings.

SAUSAGE-YAM SKILLET

1 pound bulk pork sausage
1 13½-ounce can pineapple chunks
¼ cup brown sugar
2 tablespoons lemon juice
2 teaspoons cornstarch
1 18-ounce can sweet potatoes, drained

Brown meat slowly; drain off fat. Drain pineapple; reserve syrup. Add syrup, brown sugar, and lemon juice to meat. Mix cornstarch and 2 tablespoons cold water; add to meat. Cook and stir till bubbly. Add pineapple and potatoes. Cover; cook 5 minutes. Serves 4 or 5.

Create savory Oriental fare in a flash with canned meatballs. A tangy sauce, laced with pineapple tidbits and green pepper, dresses Sweet-Sour Meatballs.

JIFFY MACARONI AND BEEF

1 pound ground beef
¼ cup chopped green pepper
2 15-ounce cans macaroni and
    cheese, cut up
1 3-ounce can chopped mushrooms,
    drained (½ cup)
1 medium tomato, cut in wedges
2 ounces sharp process American
    cheese, shredded (½ cup)

Cook meat with green pepper till meat is brown and pepper is tender. Drain. Add macaroni, mushrooms, and ¾ teaspoon salt; pour into 2-quart casserole. Bake, uncovered, at 375° for 25 minutes. Top with tomato; sprinkle with cheese. Bake 10 minutes. Serves 6.

CHILI PIES

1 15-ounce can chili with beans
1 10½-ounce can chili without
    beans
  Packaged instant mashed potatoes
    (enough for 4 servings)
¼ teaspoon dried oregano leaves,
    crushed
6 tablespoons shredded sharp
    natural Cheddar cheese

Combine chilies; heat. Prepare potatoes following package directions. Stir in oregano. Divide chili among 6 individual casseroles. Spoon potatoes around edge of casseroles. Sprinkle centers with cheese. Broil 4 inches from heat for 3 minutes. Makes 6 servings.

SWEET-SOUR SCRAMBLE

- 1 pound ground beef
- 1 medium green pepper, cut in strips
- 1 cup bias-cut celery slices
- ½ cup bias-cut green onion
- ½ teaspoon salt
- 1 13½-ounce can pineapple tidbits
- 2 tablespoons cornstarch
- 1 beef bouillon cube
- 1 tablespoon soy sauce
- 1 medium tomato, peeled and cut in eighths
- 1 3-ounce can chow mein noodles

In skillet brown meat; drain off fat. Add green pepper, celery, onion, and salt; cook till vegetables are crisp-tender, about 5 minutes. Drain pineapple, reserving syrup. Blend cornstarch with reserved syrup. Dissolve bouillon cube in 1 cup boiling water. Add bouillon, cornstarch mixture, and soy sauce to meat mixture. Cook, stirring constantly, till mixture thickens and bubbles. Add pineapple and tomatoes; heat through. Serve over chow mein noodles. Makes 4 servings.

BEEF AND BISCUIT SKILLET

Biscuits bake as snow-white dumplings atop bubbly meat and vegetable mixture—

- 1 pound ground beef
- 2 teaspoons instant minced onion
- 1 10¾-ounce can beef gravy
- 1 10-ounce package frozen mixed vegetables
- 1 package refrigerated biscuits (6 biscuits)
- ¼ cup shredded sharp natural Cheddar cheese
  Paprika

In 10-inch skillet brown meat with onion; drain off fat. Stir in gravy and ½ cup water. Add ½ teaspoon salt and frozen vegetables, breaking apart. Bring to boiling. Cover; reduce heat and simmer 10 minutes. Top with biscuits; simmer, covered, 15 minutes. Sprinkle biscuits with cheese; heat till cheese melts. Sprinkle with paprika. Makes 4 servings.

SPEEDY BEEF SKILLET

- 1 10¾-ounce can condensed tomato soup
- 1 8-ounce can whole kernel corn, drained
- 2 cups frozen Basic Ground Beef*
- ½ teaspoon salt
- ¼ teaspoon dried marjoram leaves, crushed
- 4 ounces medium noodles, uncooked

In saucepan combine all ingredients but noodles. Cover and bring to boiling; reduce heat. Cook over medium heat, stirring frequently till meat is thawed, about 10 minutes. Add uncooked noodles and ½ cup water; cover and simmer till noodles are tender, about 15 minutes, stirring occasionally. Serves 4.

VEGETABLE-MEATBALL STEW

- 1 beaten egg
- ¼ cup milk
- ¾ cup soft bread crumbs
- 2 tablespoons chopped green onion
- 1 teaspoon dry mustard
- ¼ teaspoon dried thyme leaves, crushed
- 1 pound ground beef
- 2 tablespoons shortening
- 1 beef bouillon cube
- 2 tablespoons all-purpose flour
- ¼ teaspoon kitchen bouquet
- 1 16-ounce can whole carrots
- 1 16-ounce can whole onions
- 1 3-ounce can sliced mushrooms

Combine first 6 ingredients, ½ teaspoon salt, and dash pepper. Add meat; mix well. Shape into 24 balls. In skillet brown meatballs slowly in hot shortening, about 10 minutes, shaking skillet to turn meatballs.

Meanwhile, dissolve bouillon cube in 1⅓ cups boiling water; set aside. Remove meatballs from skillet; skim fat from pan drippings. Blend flour into drippings. Add bouillon. Cook and stir till thickened and bubbly. Stir in kitchen bouquet; season with salt and pepper to taste. Drain carrots, onions, and mushrooms. Add vegetables and meatballs to skillet; cover and heat through. Serves 6.

BASIC GROUND BEEF*

Prepare meat mixture ahead and freeze, then use as a shortcut on busy days to prepare many of the recipes found on these two pages—

- 2 pounds ground beef
- 1 cup chopped celery
- 1 cup chopped onion
- ½ cup chopped green pepper

In skillet cook meat with vegetables till meat is browned and vegetables are tender. Drain off excess fat. Cool quickly. Freeze in three 2-cup portions in moistureproof containers (see page 120). Seal. Makes 6 cups.

BEEF AND RICE SKILLET

Combine one 10½-ounce can condensed cream of chicken soup; 1¾ cups water; 2 cups frozen Basic Ground Beef*; one 10-ounce package frozen peas; 1 cup uncooked packaged precooked rice; and ¼ teaspoon salt. Cover and bring to boiling; reduce heat. Simmer till meat is thawed and peas and rice are tender, 15 minutes; stir often. Serves 4.

QUICK SPAGHETTI

- 1 pound ground beef
- ½ cup chopped onion
- 1 18-ounce can (2⅛ cups) tomato juice
- 1 8-ounce can tomato sauce
- ½ teaspoon sugar
- ½ teaspoon dried oregano leaves, crushed
- ¼ teaspoon garlic powder
- 1 bay leaf
  Few drops bottled hot pepper sauce
- ½ 7-ounce package spaghetti, uncooked

In large saucepan brown beef with onion. Drain off fat. Add tomato juice, next 6 ingredients, and ½ teaspoon salt. Bring to boiling; add uncooked spaghetti. Cover; simmer 25 minutes, stirring often. Remove bay leaf. Pass Parmesan cheese, if desired. Serves 5 or 6.

AMERICAN PIZZA

- 2 cups frozen Basic Ground Beef*
- 1 small clove garlic, minced
- ½ teaspoon dried oregano leaves, crushed
- ¼ teaspoon fennel seed (optional)
- 1 15½-ounce package cheese pizza mix
- 2 ounces sharp process American cheese, shredded (½ cup)

In saucepan thaw meat over low heat; cook till liquid is evaporated. Stir in seasonings. Meanwhile, prepare pizza dough following package directions. Roll or pat out to fit 12-inch pizza pan. Crimp edges. Spread pizza sauce (from package mix) over dough. Top with meat, American cheese, then grated cheese (from package mix). Bake at 425° for 25 to 30 minutes. Makes one 12-inch pizza.

EASY LASAGNE

- 4 ounces lasagne noodles
- 1 2½-ounce envelope spaghetti sauce mix with tomato
- 2 cups frozen Basic Ground Beef*
- 1 12-ounce carton (1½ cups) cream-style cottage cheese
- 1 6-ounce package sliced mozzarella cheese (4 slices)

Cook noodles in boiling salted water following package directions; drain. Prepare sauce following package directions. Add frozen meat. Cover; cook over low heat till thawed, about 10 minutes. In greased 10x6x1½-inch baking dish, layer *one-half each* noodles (cut to fit), cottage cheese, mozzarella, then sauce. Repeat layers. Bake at 375° for 30 minutes. Let stand 10 minutes. Makes 4 servings.

QUICK CHILI ON BUNS

Combine one 15-ounce can chili with beans; one 10¾-ounce can condensed tomato soup; 2 cups frozen Basic Ground Beef*; and ½ cup chili sauce. Cover; cook over medium heat till meat thaws, about 10 minutes. Serve over 8 hamburger buns, split and toasted. Serves 8.

Hamburgers and Sandwiches

BASIC HAMBURGERS

Skillet: Shape 1 pound ground beef into 4 patties, ¾ inch thick. Heat skillet sizzling hot; sprinkle skillet lightly with salt. Cook burgers over medium-high heat 5 minutes; turn and cook 4 to 5 minutes longer. Partially cover if meat spatters.

Broiler: Combine 1 pound ground beef, ½ teaspoon salt, dash pepper, and ¼ cup finely chopped onion (optional). Shape into 4 patties, ¾ inch thick. Broil 3 inches from heat 6 minutes. Turn; broil 4 minutes or till done.

IOWA CORN BURGERS

As pictured opposite chapter introduction—

    1 8-ounce can whole kernel corn
    ¼ cup catsup
    1 tablespoon grated onion
    1 tablespoon snipped parsley
    1½ pounds ground beef
    8 hamburger buns, split and
         toasted

Drain corn. Mix first 4 ingredients, 1 teaspoon salt, and ⅛ teaspoon pepper. Add beef; mix well. Shape into 8 patties, ¾ inch thick. Broil 3 inches from heat 6 minutes. Turn; broil 4 to 6 minutes. Serve in buns. Serves 8.

MUSHROOM BURGERS

Combine ½ cup buttermilk or sour milk; ⅓ cup fine dry bread crumbs; one 3-ounce can chopped mushrooms, drained (½ cup); 2 teaspoons instant minced onion; and 1 teaspoon seasoned salt. Add 1 pound ground beef; mix well. Shape into 6 patties, ¾ inch thick. Broil 3 inches from heat 6 minutes. Turn; broil 4 to 6 minutes longer. Serve in 6 hamburger buns, split and toasted. Serves 6.

3-DECKER BURGERS

    ¼ cup milk
    ¼ cup fine dry bread crumbs
    1 pound ground beef
    4 slices process Swiss cheese
    4 slices boiled ham
    4 hamburger buns, split and
         toasted

Combine milk and crumbs. Add beef; mix well. Shape mixture into 12 thin patties. Trim cheese and ham to fit patties. On one patty place cheese slice; top with second patty, ham slice, then third patty. Seal edges. Repeat for each burger with remaining patties, cheese, and ham. Broil 3 inches from heat for 6 minutes. Turn; broil 4 to 6 minutes longer. Serve in buns. Makes 4 servings.

SMOKY CHEESEBURGERS

    ¾ cup chopped onion
    2 tablespoons salad oil
    1½ pounds ground beef
    ¾ teaspoon salt
         Dash pepper
    1 5-ounce jar process cheese
         spread with smoke flavor,
         softened
    1 tablespoon pickle relish
    1 teaspoon prepared mustard
    6 hamburger buns, split

Cook onion in hot oil till tender. Combine with beef, salt, and pepper; mix well. Shape into 6 patties. Panbroil in hot skillet over medium-high heat for 5 minutes. Turn; cook 4 to 5 minutes longer or till done.

Combine cheese spread, pickle relish, and mustard. Spread 1 tablespoon mixture on each bun half. Broil buns 1 to 1½ minutes or till bun toasts and cheese bubbles. Serve patties in buns. Makes 6 servings.

When stuffing burgers such as Blue Cheese Burgers, leave a margin for sealing to prevent loss of filling during cooking.

BLUE CHEESE BURGERS

1 beaten egg
1 pound ground beef
2 ounces blue cheese, crumbled
  (½ cup)
2 tablespoons mayonnaise
1 tablespoon Worcestershire sauce
½ teaspoon dry mustard
4 hamburger buns, split, toasted,
  and buttered

Combine egg, ¼ teaspoon salt, and dash pepper. Add beef; mix well. Shape into 8 patties, ¼ inch thick. Blend blue cheese with next 3 ingredients. Spoon mixture atop *four* patties, leaving ½-inch margin around edges. Top with remaining patties; seal. Broil 3 inches from heat 6 minutes. Turn; broil 4 to 6 minutes. Serve in buns. Makes 4 servings.

OLIVE BURGERS

Combine ⅓ cup tomato juice; ¼ cup quick-cooking rolled oats; ¼ cup sliced pimiento-stuffed green olives; 2 tablespoons chopped onion; and ¼ teaspoon salt. Add 1 pound ground beef; mix well. Shape into 6 patties, ¾ inch thick. Broil 3 inches from heat 6 minutes. Turn; broil 4 to 6 minutes. Serve in 6 hamburger buns, split. Serves 6.

ONION BURGERS

Make use of leftover chip dip—

Combine ½ cup sour cream-onion dip; 3 tablespoons fine dry bread crumbs; ¼ teaspoon salt; and dash pepper. Add 1 pound ground beef; mix well. Shape into 4 patties, ¾ inch thick. Broil 3 inches from heat 6 minutes. Turn; broil 4 to 6 minutes. Serve in 4 hamburger buns, split and toasted. Serves 4.

OPEN-FACE BURGERS

1 cup dairy sour cream
¼ cup finely chopped onion
2 teaspoons Worcestershire sauce
2 pounds ground beef
2 beef bouillon cubes
1 cup dairy sour cream
2 tablespoons finely snipped
  parsley
4 hamburger buns, split and
  toasted

Combine first 3 ingredients, 1 teaspoon salt, and dash pepper. Add beef; mix well. Shape into 8 patties. Broil 3 inches from heat 6 minutes. Turn; broil 4 to 6 minutes longer.

Meanwhile, dissolve bouillon in ¼ cup boiling water. Stir in sour cream and parsley. Heat; *do not boil.* Place patties on bun halves; top with sour cream sauce. Serves 8.

Clouds of tangy sour cream sauce flecked with parsley swirl atop Open-Face Burgers served on toasted bun halves.

ORANGE-TOPPED BURGERS

As shown opposite chapter introduction—

   ½ cup dairy sour cream
   2 tablespoons chopped green onion
   1 teaspoon Worcestershire sauce
1½ pounds ground beef
   2 large oranges, peeled and
      cut into 6 slices each
   1 medium green pepper, cut into
      6 rings
   6 hamburger buns, split and
      toasted

Combine first 3 ingredients and ¾ teaspoon salt. Add meat; mix well. Shape into 6 patties. Broil 3 inches from heat for 6 minutes. Turn; broil 4 to 6 minutes longer. Top each with 2 orange slices and green pepper ring. Broil 2 minutes longer or till meat is done. Serve in buns. Makes 6 servings.

CUCUMBER BURGERS

Shred enough of 1 medium unpeeled cucumber to measure ½ cup; drain thoroughly. Stir in ½ cup dairy sour cream, ¼ cup chopped onion, 1 teaspoon salt, 1 teaspoon lemon juice, and dash pepper. Add 1½ pounds ground beef; mix well. Chill. Shape into 6 patties, ¾ inch thick. Broil 3 inches from heat 6 minutes. Turn; broil 4 minutes. Serve in 6 hamburger buns, split. Serves 6.

BANANA BURGERS

   1 beaten egg
   ¼ teaspoon ground cinnamon
   1 pound ground beef
   1 small banana
   4 frankfurter buns, split
      and toasted

Combine egg, 1 teaspoon salt, and cinnamon. Add meat; mix well. Cut banana in half crosswise, then in half lengthwise. Divide meat into 4 portions; shape each portion around banana quarter. Broil 3 inches from heat for 12 minutes, turning ¼ turn every 3 minutes. Serve in buns. Makes 4 servings.

ORIENTAL CRUNCH BURGERS

   2 pounds ground beef
1½ teaspoons salt
   1 5-ounce can bean sprouts,
      drained
   1 5-ounce can water chestnuts,
      drained and chopped
   ¼ cup chopped green onion
   2 tablespoons soy sauce
   8 hamburger buns, split and
      toasted

Mix meat with salt; shape into 16 thin patties, 4 inches in diameter. Combine bean sprouts, water chestnuts, onion, and soy sauce. Toss together lightly. Place about 2 tablespoons mixture on *eight* of the patties. Cover with remaining patties; seal edges. Broil 3 inches from heat for 6 minutes; turn and broil 6 minutes longer or till done. Serve in toasted hamburger buns. Makes 8 servings.

COTTAGE CHEESE BURGERS

Combine 1 beaten egg; one 8-ounce carton (1 cup) cream-style cottage cheese with chives; ½ teaspoon seasoned salt; and ½ teaspoon Worcestershire sauce. Add 1½ pounds ground beef; mix well. Shape into 8 patties, ¾ inch thick. Panbroil in hot skillet over medium heat 5 to 7 minutes. Turn; panbroil 4 to 5 minutes longer. Partially cover if meat spatters. Serve in 8 hamburger buns, split and toasted. Makes 8 servings.

BEEF PLUS BURGERS

   1 cup nonfat dry milk powder
   ¼ cup cold water
   1 beaten egg
   1 tablespoon instant minced onion
1½ pounds ground beef
   6 hamburger buns, split and
      toasted

Blend dry milk with water; stir in egg, onion, and 1 teaspoon salt. Add meat; mix well. Shape into 6 patties, ¾ inch thick. Broil 3 inches from heat 6 minutes. Turn; broil 4 to 6 minutes longer. Serve in buns. Serves 6.

GUACAMOLE BURGERS

> 1 beaten egg
> 1 teaspoon salt
> ⅛ teaspoon pepper
> 1½ pounds ground beef
>   Guacamole Stuffing
> 4 hamburger buns, split and
>   toasted

Combine egg, salt, and pepper. Add meat; mix well. Shape into 8 patties, ½ inch thick. Top *four* of the patties with Guacamole Stuffing, leaving ½ inch around edge. Cover with remaining patties; seal edges. Broil 3 inches from heat 8 minutes. Turn; broil 8 minutes or till done. Serve in buns. Makes 4 servings.

Guacamole Stuffing: Mash 1 avocado, pitted and peeled (1 cup). Stir in 1 tomato, peeled and chopped (¾ cup); 1 tablespoon grated onion; 2 teaspoons lemon juice; ½ teaspoon salt; and ¼ teaspoon chili powder.

PINEAPPLE BURGERS

> 1 8¾-ounce can crushed pineapple,
>   drained
> ¼ cup chopped green pepper
> 2 tablespoons soy sauce
> ½ teaspoon salt
> 1½ pounds ground beef
> 6 hamburger buns, split and
>   toasted

Combine crushed pineapple, green pepper, soy sauce, and salt. Add meat and mix thoroughly. Shape into 6 patties. Broil 3 inches from heat for 6 minutes. Turn; broil 4 to 6 minutes longer or till done. Serve in toasted hamburger buns. Makes 6 servings.

BEEF AND CARROT BURGERS

Combine 1 beaten egg; 2 tablespoons milk; 1 cup finely chopped raw carrot; 1 teaspoon seasoned salt; and dash pepper. Add 1½ pounds ground beef; mix well. Shape into 6 patties, ¾ inch thick. Broil 3 inches from heat for 6 minutes. Turn; broil 4 minutes longer or till done. Serve in 6 hamburger buns, split and toasted. Makes 6 servings.

TREASURE LOGS

Burger oozes with filling and looks like a hot dog—

> 1 beaten egg
> 1 teaspoon Worcestershire sauce
> ¾ teaspoon salt
> 1 pound ground beef
> 1 3-ounce can chopped mushrooms,
>   drained and finely chopped
> 2 tablespoons chopped green onion
> 2 slices process Swiss cheese,
>   cut in ¾-inch strips
> 4 frankfurter buns, split and
>   toasted

Combine egg, Worcestershire sauce, and salt. Add meat; mix well. Divide mixture into 4 portions. On waxed paper pat each portion into a 5x4-inch rectangle. Leaving ½-inch margin, top each burger with *one-fourth each* of the mushrooms, onion, and cheese strips. Lifting edge of waxed paper, fold meat over filling pressing along edges to seal. Broil logs 3 inches from heat for 6 minutes. Turn; broil 4 to 6 minutes longer. Serve logs in toasted buns. Makes 4 servings.

APPLESAUCE BURGERS

Combine 1 beaten egg; ½ cup applesauce; 1 cup soft bread crumbs (1½ slices); ¼ cup finely chopped onion; 1 teaspoon salt; and 1½ teaspoons Dijon-style mustard. Add 1½ pounds ground beef; mix thoroughly. Shape into 6 patties, ¾ inch thick. Broil 3 inches from heat for 6 minutes. Turn; broil 4 to 6 minutes or till done. Serve in 6 hamburger buns, split and toasted. Makes 6 servings.

CHEESE AND BEEF BURGERS

Combine ¼ cup catsup; 1 tablespoon finely chopped onion; and ½ teaspoon dry mustard. Add 4 ounces sharp process American cheese, shredded (1 cup), and 1 pound ground beef; mix well. Shape into 4 patties, ¾ inch thick. Panbroil in 1 tablespoon hot salad oil in skillet over medium-low heat for 6 minutes. Turn; cook 5 to 6 minutes longer. Serve in 4 hamburger buns, split and toasted. Serves 4.

DEVILED HAMBURGERS

Combine ⅓ cup chili sauce, 1 tablespoon chopped onion, 1 teaspoon prepared mustard, 1 teaspoon prepared horseradish, ½ teaspoon Worcestershire sauce, and ¾ teaspoon salt. Add 1 pound ground beef; mix well. Trim crusts from 8 slices bread; toast one side. Spread each untoasted side with ¼ cup meat; spread to edges. Broil 5 to 6 minutes. Serves 4.

JIFFY PICKLEBURGERS

- 1 beaten egg
- ¼ cup finely chopped onion
- 1 teaspoon prepared horseradish
- 1 teaspoon Worcestershire sauce
- ½ teaspoon celery salt
- 1 pound ground beef
- 3 4-inch dill pickles, halved lengthwise
- 6 frankfurter buns, split, toasted, and buttered

Combine first 5 ingredients, ¼ teaspoon salt, and dash pepper. Add beef; mix well. Divide into 6 portions; shape around pickles. Broil 3 inches from heat 6 minutes. Turn; broil 4 to 6 minutes. Serve in buns. Serves 6.

GERMAN BURGERS

As pictured opposite chapter introduction—

- 1½ pounds ground beef
- 1 tablespoon caraway seed
- 12 slices rye bread, toasted
- 1 cup coleslaw, drained

Combine beef, caraway, 1 teaspoon salt, and ⅛ teaspoon pepper; mix well. Shape into 6 patties, ¾ inch thick. Panbroil in hot skillet over medium-high heat 5 minutes. Turn; cook 4 to 5 minutes more. Place each patty on rye slice. Divide coleslaw and spoon atop; top with remaining bread. Makes 6 servings.

NUTTY BURGERS

- 1 pound ground beef
- ¼ cup chopped peanuts
- 4 hamburger buns, split and toasted

Combine beef, peanuts, ½ teaspoon salt, and dash pepper; mix well. Shape into 4 patties, ¾ inch thick. Panbroil in hot skillet over medium-high heat 5 minutes. Turn; cook 4 to 5 minutes longer. Serve in buns. Serves 4.

Juicy burger wraps around dill pickle strip for a surprise-in-a-bun. Pass catsup and mustard to brighten Jiffy Pickleburgers. Accompany with potato chips.

Meatballs needn't be confined to spaghetti. Saucy meatballs peek from frankfurter buns in Meatball Heroes—perfect for the teen-age crowd after the game.

MEATBALL HEROES

    2 tablespoons salad oil
    ½ clove garlic, minced
    1 8-ounce can tomato sauce
    ¼ cup dry onion soup mix
    1 teaspoon sugar
    ½ teaspoon dried oregano leaves,
        crushed
    ½ cup milk
    ⅓ cup fine dry bread crumbs
    1 pound ground beef
    2 tablespoons salad oil
    8 frankfurter buns, split and
        toasted

In saucepan heat first 2 ingredients together; stir in next 4 ingredients and 1 cup water. Gently boil, uncovered, 10 to 15 minutes; stir occasionally till slightly thickened.

Combine milk, crumbs, ½ teaspoon salt, and dash pepper. Add meat; mix well. Shape into 24 small balls; brown in hot salad oil. Add to sauce; cook, covered, 20 minutes. Serve 3 meatballs with sauce in each frankfurter bun. Makes 8 servings.

CHEESE-TOPPED BURGERS

Combine 2 pounds ground beef; 1 tablespoon bottled steak sauce; 1 teaspoon Worcestershire sauce; ¾ teaspoon salt; ¼ teaspoon bottled hot pepper sauce; and dash pepper. Mix well. Shape into 8 patties, ½ inch thick. Broil 3 inches from heat 6 minutes. Turn; broil 4 minutes. Toss 3 ounces sharp process American cheese, shredded (¾ cup), with ¼ cup finely chopped onion; sprinkle atop burgers. Heat in broiler till cheese melts. Serve in 8 hamburger buns, split and toasted. Serves 8.

BACON BURGERS

Perk-up burger flavor with smoky bacon bits—

Cook 4 slices bacon till crisp; drain and crumble. Combine with 1 pound ground beef, ½ teaspoon salt, and dash pepper; mix well. Shape into 4 patties, ¾ inch thick. Broil 3 inches from heat 6 minutes. Turn; broil 4 minutes longer or till done. Serve in 4 hamburger buns, split and toasted. Serves 4.

PIZZA BY-THE-YARD

1 unsliced loaf French bread
1 6-ounce can tomato paste
⅓ cup grated Parmesan cheese
¼ cup finely chopped onion
¼ cup chopped pitted ripe olives
½ teaspoon dried oregano leaves, crushed
1 pound ground beef
4 tomatoes, sliced (16 slices)
1 8-ounce package sliced sharp process American cheese

Cut loaf in half lengthwise. Combine tomato paste, next 4 ingredients, ¾ teaspoon salt, and ⅛ teaspoon pepper. Add meat; mix well. Spread atop loaf halves. Place on baking sheet. Bake at 400° for 20 minutes. Remove from oven; top with tomato slices. Cut cheese in 1-inch strips. Crisscross strips atop tomatoes. Bake 5 minutes. Serves 4 or 5.

SAUCY BEEF BOAT

For individual boats, use hollowed out hard rolls—

1 unsliced loaf French bread
1 pound ground beef
½ cup chopped onion
1 8-ounce can tomato sauce
1 1½-ounce envelope spaghetti sauce mix
¼ cup sliced pitted ripe olives

Cut thin slice from top of loaf; set aside. Scoop out bottom, leaving ½-inch shell. Tear bread in small pieces; reserve. Brown meat with onion; drain. Add remaining ingredients and 1 cup water. Bring to boiling; reduce heat. Simmer, uncovered, 5 minutes; stir occasionally. Stir in reserved bread.

Spoon mixture into shell. Place on baking sheet. Bake at 350° for 18 to 20 minutes. Heat top in oven last 5 minutes. To serve, place top on loaf; slice crosswise. Serves 6.

← Man-sized sandwiches can be fun to prepare and eat when they are as bright and robust as Stroganoff Sandwich or as quick and easy as Meat Loaf Splits.

STROGANOFF SANDWICH

1 unsliced loaf French bread
1 pound ground beef
¼ cup chopped green onion
1 cup dairy sour cream
1 tablespoon milk
1 teaspoon Worcestershire sauce
⅛ teaspoon garlic powder
Butter or margarine, softened
2 tomatoes, sliced
1 green pepper, cut in rings
4 ounces sharp process American cheese, shredded (1 cup)

Cut loaf in half lengthwise; wrap in foil. Heat at 375° for 10 to 15 minutes. In skillet cook beef with onion till meat is browned; drain off fat. Stir in sour cream, next 3 ingredients, and ¾ teaspoon salt; heat, *but do not boil.* Butter cut surfaces of bread.

Spread half of *hot* meat mixture on each loaf half. Arrange tomato slices alternately with green pepper rings atop meat. Sprinkle with cheese. Place on baking sheet; bake at 375° for 5 minutes. Makes 8 servings.

MEAT LOAF SPLITS

Split sandwich at center for easier eating—

1 unsliced loaf Italian or French bread
¼ cup butter, softened
⅛ teaspoon garlic powder
8 slices process American cheese
4 slices leftover meat loaf, sliced ⅜ inch thick
Grated Parmesan cheese

Cut ends from loaf; store for later use. Slice loaf crosswise into 8 pieces. In each piece make 3 slashes, *almost to bottom.*

Blend butter with garlic; spread on all cut surfaces of bread. Quarter cheese and meat slices. Place meat slice between 2 cheese slices; repeat to make 16 meat-cheese stacks.

Insert stacks in the *two* end slashes in each bread piece. Sprinkle sides of sandwiches with Parmesan cheese. Place on baking sheet. Bake at 400° for 8 to 10 minutes or till lightly browned. Makes 8 servings.

BARBECUED SAUSAGE

1 pound bulk pork sausage
⅓ cup chopped onion
1 8-ounce can tomato sauce
1 tablespoon sugar
2 tablespoons catsup
1 tablespoon vinegar
1 tablespoon Worcestershire sauce
6 hamburger buns, split, toasted, and buttered

Brown meat with onion, breaking up meat; drain. Add tomato sauce, next 4 ingredients, ½ cup water, and ¼ teaspoon salt. Simmer, covered, 30 minutes. Serve in buns. Serves 6.

BARBECUE BURGERS

1 pound ground beef
¾ cup chopped celery
½ cup chopped onion
¼ cup chopped green pepper
¾ cup chili sauce
¾ cup catsup
10 hamburger buns, split and toasted

In skillet brown beef with vegetables till vegetables are crisp-tender; drain. Add chili sauce, catsup, ¼ teaspoon salt, and dash pepper. Simmer, covered, 20 minutes; stir occasionally. Serve in buns. Serves 10.

SPICY BEEF BARBECUE

1 pound ground beef
2 cups shredded cabbage
½ cup catsup
½ cup beef broth
2 teaspoons lemon juice
2 teaspoons Worcestershire sauce
1 teaspoon prepared horseradish
1 teaspoon prepared mustard
8 hamburger buns, split and toasted

In skillet brown meat; drain off fat. Add cabbage, next 6 ingredients, and ¼ teaspoon salt. Cover; simmer 20 minutes. Uncover; cook 10 minutes. Serve in buns. Serves 8.

OPEN-FACE RYE BURGERS

1 pound ground beef
⅓ cup bottled barbecue sauce *or* catsup
¼ cup chopped onion
8 slices rye bread
8 slices process American cheese
16 thin green pepper rings

Combine first 3 ingredients and ¼ teaspoon salt; mix well. Toast bread on one side. Spread ¼ cup meat on untoasted side of each slice; spread evenly and completely to edges. Broil 3 inches from heat 5 to 6 minutes. Remove from heat; top with cheese slices and pepper rings. Return to boiler 1 minute or till cheese melts. Makes 8 servings.

SAUCY BEAN BURGERS

1 pound ground beef
1 11½-ounce can condensed bean with bacon soup
½ cup catsup
¼ cup water
8 hamburger buns, split and toasted

In skillet brown beef; drain. Add soup, catsup, and water. Cook and stir till boiling, about 5 minutes. Serve in buns. Serves 8.

CHILI-BURGER RAREBIT

1 15-ounce can chili with beans
4 ounces process American cheese, shredded (1 cup)
2 to 3 tablespoons red Burgundy *or* water
1 pound ground beef
4 bias-cut slices French bread, 1 inch thick

In saucepan mix chili, ½ *cup* of the cheese, and wine. Heat and stir till cheese melts. Shape beef into 4 patties, ¾ inch thick; cook in skillet over medium-high heat 4 to 6 minutes. Turn; season with salt. Cook 4 to 6 minutes. Serve on bread; top with chili. Sprinkle with remaining cheese. Serves 4.

YANKEE TOSTADAS*

¾ pound ground beef
¼ cup chopped onion
1 cup bottled barbecue sauce
½ teaspoon dried oregano
   leaves, crushed
½ teaspoon garlic salt
1 11-ounce can baked beans in
   molasses sauce
8 toaster-style corn muffins
1½ cups shredded lettuce
4 ounces sharp natural Cheddar
   cheese, shredded (1 cup)

Brown beef with onion; drain. Add next 3 ingredients; simmer 5 minutes. In saucepan heat beans. Toast muffins; top each with 3 tablespoons beans, 3 tablespoons lettuce, ¼ cup meat, and 2 tablespoons cheese. Serves 8.

*For *Jiffy Tostadas* omit first 3 ingredients. Heat one 15-ounce can barbecue sauce and beef; add seasonings and dash red pepper.

CRUNCHY TACOS

2 cups shredded cabbage
2 teaspoons vinegar
2 teaspoons salad oil
½ teaspoon sugar
½ teaspoon salt
½ pound ground beef
½ cup chopped onion
1 16-ounce can tomatoes, cut up
12 frozen or canned tortillas
   Salad oil

Combine first 5 ingredients; toss together. Set aside. In skillet brown beef with onion; drain off fat. Drain cut-up tomatoes, reserving ¼ cup juice. Add tomatoes and reserved ¼ cup juice to meat and onion; heat through.

Meanwhile, fry tortillas in hot oil till crisp and golden, holding two edges together (but not tight) with tongs. Drain; fill immediately. Spoon some meat mixture and some cabbage into each taco. Makes 12 tacos.

Revive south-of-the-border flavor with spicy-hot Yankee Tostadas. For an even faster sandwich when time is short, serve Jiffy Tostadas using canned meat sauce.

TOMATO-CHEESE BURGERS

1½ pounds ground beef
¼ cup butter or margarine
¼ cup all-purpose flour
2 cups milk
6 ounces sharp process American
    cheese, shredded (1½ cups)
1 teaspoon Worcestershire sauce
6 slices white bread, toasted *or*
    3 English muffins, split and
    toasted
6 slices tomato

Mix beef with ¾ teaspoon salt; shape into 6 patties, ¾ inch thick. Broil 3 inches from heat 6 minutes. Turn; broil 4 to 6 minutes more. Meanwhile, in saucepan melt butter; blend in flour and ¼ teaspoon salt. Add milk; cook and stir till bubbly. Add cheese and Worcestershire; stir till cheese melts. Place patties on bread; top with tomato. Pour cheese sauce over. Makes 6 servings.

GROUND BEEF REUBEN

½ pound ground beef
2 tablespoons chopped onion
⅓ cup thousand island salad
    dressing
12 slices pumpernickel bread
¾ cup drained sauerkraut, snipped
6 slices process Swiss cheese
6 tablespoons butter, softened

In skillet brown meat with onion; drain. Stir in salad dressing. Spread on *six* slices bread; top each with 2 tablespoons sauerkraut, 1 slice cheese, then remaining bread. Butter tops and bottoms of sandwiches. Grill on both sides till cheese melts. Serves 6.

BEEF SALAD SANDWICHES

Mix 1½ cups ground cooked roast beef; ⅓ cup mayonnaise; 1 tablespoon pickle relish, drained; 1 tablespoon finely chopped onion; 1 teaspoon prepared mustard; and ¼ teaspoon salt. Spread 8 slices bread with softened butter. Spread meat on *four* slices. Top with lettuce, then remaining bread. Serves 4.

HAM TRIPLE-DECKERS

1½ cups ground fully-cooked ham
2 hard-cooked eggs, chopped
2 tablespoons chopped green pepper
1 tablespoon prepared mustard
3 tablespoons mayonnaise
12 slices white bread
    Butter or margarine, softened

Combine first 4 ingredients; mix well. Stir in mayonnaise. Spread one side of each slice bread with butter. Spread *half* of the ham mixture on *four* slices, spreading to edges. Cover each with second slice. Spread remaining ham on second bread slices. Top with remaining bread, buttered side down.

Melt a little additional butter; brush on outside slices of sandwiches. Place sandwiches on baking sheet; bake at 375° for 15 to 20 minutes or till golden brown. Serves 4.

CARAWAY AND HAM-WICHES

¼ cup chopped onion
1 tablespoon butter
1 cup ground fully-cooked ham
4 ounces sharp natural Cheddar
    cheese, shredded (1 cup)
1 tablespoon prepared mustard
1 teaspoon caraway seed
8 hamburger buns, split and
    toasted

Cook onion in butter till tender; stir in ham, cheese, mustard, and caraway. Spread on buns. Wrap separately in foil; heat at 400° for 15 to 20 minutes. Serves 8.

HAM-MARMALADE SPREAD

1 cup ground fully-cooked ham
¼ cup mayonnaise or salad dressing
1 tablespoon orange marmalade
2 teaspoons prepared mustard
8 slices rye bread, buttered
    Lettuce

Combine first 4 ingredients; mix well. Spread on *four* slices bread; top with lettuce, then remaining bread. Makes 4 sandwiches.

LONG HAM QUICKNICS

- 1 beaten egg
- ⅓ cup milk
- ½ cup soft bread crumbs
- ¼ cup finely chopped green pepper
- ¼ cup finely chopped onion
- 2 tablespoons brown sugar
- 3 cups ground fully-cooked ham
- 2 tablespoons butter, melted
- ¼ cup mayonnaise or salad dressing
- ¼ cup prepared mustard
- 8 frankfurter buns, split and toasted

Blend first 6 ingredients and dash pepper. Add ham; mix well. Shape into 8 rolls the size of frankfurters. Place in 12x7½x2-inch baking dish; drizzle with butter. Bake at 400° for 20 to 25 minutes. Blend mayonnaise with mustard. Serve ham rolls in buns. Pass mustard sauce. Makes 8 sandwiches.

PINEAPPLE-HAM SPREAD

Mix 1 cup ground fully-cooked ham; one 8½-ounce can crushed pineapple, *well* drained; ⅓ cup mayonnaise; 1 tablespoon brown sugar; and 1 teaspoon prepared mustard. Spread 12 slices rye bread with softened butter. Spread ham on *six* slices; top with lettuce, then remaining bread. Serves 6.

CHEESY-HAM BUNS

- 1 cup ground fully-cooked ham
- 4 ounces process American cheese, shredded (1 cup)
- 1 hard-cooked egg, chopped
- 2 tablespoons thinly sliced pimiento-stuffed green olives
- 2 tablespoons chopped green onion
- ¼ cup chili sauce
- 2 tablespoons mayonnaise
- 6 frankfurter buns, split

Combine first 5 ingredients; blend chili sauce with mayonnaise. Add to meat mixture; mix well. Spoon into buns. Wrap separately in foil; twist ends securely. Heat at 400° for 15 minutes. Makes 6 sandwiches.

TURKEY BURGERS

- ¼ cup chopped onion
- 1 tablespoon butter
- 1 tablespoon all-purpose flour
- 1 chicken bouillon cube, crumbled
- ½ cup milk
- 1 beaten egg
- ½ cup soft bread crumbs
- ⅛ teaspoon dried rosemary leaves, crushed
- 3 cups ground or finely chopped cooked turkey
- 1 tablespoon salad oil
- 5 hamburger buns, split, toasted, and buttered
- 1 8-ounce can whole cranberry sauce
- Shredded lettuce

In saucepan cook onion in butter till tender; blend in flour. Add bouillon cube and milk. Cook and stir till bubbly; set aside. Combine egg, crumbs, and rosemary. Add turkey and onion sauce; mix well. Shape into 5 patties. Brown in hot oil in skillet over medium heat 3 to 4 minutes on each side. Place patties on bottom halves of buns; top with cranberry sauce and shredded lettuce. Cover with bun tops. Makes 5 sandwiches.

TURKEY SALADWICHES

Mix 2 cups ground cooked turkey; ½ cup chopped celery; 2 tablespoons chopped onion; 2 ounces sharp process American cheese, diced (½ cup); 2 hard-cooked eggs, chopped; and ½ cup mayonnaise. Spread 8 hamburger buns, split, with softened butter. Spread meat mixture on buns. Wrap buns separately in foil. Heat at 400° for 20 minutes. Serves 8.

CHICKEN SANDWICHES

Mix 1 cup ground cooked chicken *or* turkey; 1 hard-cooked egg, chopped; ⅓ cup chopped celery; ⅓ cup mayonnaise; 2 tablespoons drained pickle relish; and ¼ teaspoon salt. Spread 12 slices bread with softened butter. Spread meat mixture on *six* slices; top with remaining bread. Makes 6 sandwiches.

Soups for the Main Course

CHILI CON CARNE

Pass corn chips, freshly chopped onion, or shredded cheese as toppers—

1 pound ground beef
1 cup chopped onion
¾ cup chopped green pepper
1 16-ounce can tomatoes, cut up
1 16-ounce can kidney beans, drained
1 8-ounce can tomato sauce
1 teaspoon salt
1 to 2 teaspoons chili powder
1 bay leaf

In skillet cook meat, onion, and green pepper till meat is browned and vegetables are tender. Drain off fat. Stir in tomatoes, beans, tomato sauce, salt, chili powder, and bay leaf. Cover and simmer for 1 hour. Remove bay leaf. Makes 4 servings.

CHEESEBURGER CHOWDER

1 pound ground beef
½ cup finely chopped celery
¼ cup chopped onion
2 tablespoons chopped green pepper
3 tablespoons all-purpose flour
½ teaspoon salt
4 cups milk
1 tablespoon beef-flavored gravy base
4 ounces sharp natural Cheddar cheese, shredded (1 cup)

Brown beef in large skillet. Drain off fat. Add celery, onion, and green pepper; cook till vegetables are tender. Blend in flour and salt; add milk and gravy base. Cook and stir over low heat till thickened and bubbly. Add cheese; cook and stir just till cheese melts. Makes 4 to 6 servings.

SAUSAGE-VEGETABLE SOUP

1 pound bulk pork sausage
2 medium raw potatoes, peeled and cubed (2 cups)
¼ cup chopped onion
¾ teaspoon salt
⅛ teaspoon pepper
1 18-ounce can tomato juice
1 8¾-ounce can whole kernel corn, undrained
½ cup milk
1 tablespoon all-purpose flour

In large saucepan brown sausage. Drain off fat. Add potatoes, onion, 1 cup water, salt, and pepper. Cover and simmer 20 minutes or till potatoes are tender. Add tomato juice and corn. Blend milk with flour; stir into soup. Cook and stir over low heat till thickened and bubbly. Makes 6 servings.

BEEF AND CORN CHOWDER

1 pound ground beef
½ cup chopped onion
2 medium raw potatoes, peeled and cut in ¼-inch cubes (2 cups)
1 cup thinly sliced celery
1 chicken bouillon cube, crushed
3 cups milk
1 17-ounce can cream-style corn
¼ teaspoon dried thyme leaves, crushed
2 tablespoons snipped parsley

Cook beef and onion in Dutch oven till meat is browned. Drain off fat. Add potatoes, celery, 1 cup water, 1½ teaspoons salt, and bouillon cube. Cook, covered, 15 minutes or till vegetables are tender. Add milk, corn, and thyme. Heat mixture just to boiling. Season to taste with salt and pepper. Before serving stir in parsley. Makes 8 to 10 servings.

CHILI WITH LIMAS

   1 pound ground beef
   2 10¾-ounce cans condensed
      tomato soup
   1 17-ounce can lima beans,
      undrained
   1 17-ounce can whole kernel corn,
      undrained
   1 cup chopped celery
  ½ cup chopped green pepper
  ½ cup chopped onion
   2 teaspoons chili powder

Brown meat in large skillet. Drain off fat. Stir in remaining ingredients, ½ teaspoon salt, and dash pepper. Simmer, covered, 1 hour, stirring occasionally. Serve in bowls. Serves 6.

BEEF AND RICE SOUP

   1 pound ground beef
   1 28-ounce can tomatoes, cut up
  ½ cup uncooked long-grain rice
   1 cup chopped celery
   2 tablespoons chopped green pepper
   1 envelope dry onion soup mix
   3 beef bouillon cubes
  ½ teaspoon dried basil leaves,
      crushed

In large saucepan brown meat. Drain off fat. Stir in 4 cups water, ¼ teaspoon salt, and remaining ingredients. Bring to boiling. Reduce heat; cover and simmer 20 minutes. Stir occasionally. Makes 8 servings.

VEGETABLE-BURGER SOUP

  ½ pound ground beef
   1 16-ounce can stewed tomatoes
   1 8-ounce can tomato sauce
   1 10-ounce package frozen mixed
      vegetables
  ¼ cup dry onion soup mix
   1 teaspoon sugar

In large saucepan brown meat. Drain off fat. Stir in 2 cups water and remaining ingredients. Bring to boiling. Reduce heat; cover and simmer 20 minutes. Makes 6 to 8 servings.

HAMBURGER SOUP

Perfect for lunch on a cold day—

   1 pound ground beef
   1 cup chopped onion
  ½ cup chopped green pepper
   1 18-ounce can tomato juice
   1 cup sliced raw carrots
   1 beef bouillon cube
   1 teaspoon seasoned salt
  ½ teaspoon salt
   1 cup diced raw potatoes
   2 tablespoons snipped parsley
  ⅓ cup all-purpose flour
   4 cups milk

Brown meat in Dutch oven. Drain off fat. Add onion and green pepper; cook till vegetables are crisp-tender. Stir in tomato juice, carrots, bouillon cube, seasonings, and ⅛ teaspoon pepper. Cover; simmer about 10 minutes. Add potatoes and parsley; cover and cook 15 minutes or till vegetables are tender. Blend flour with *1 cup* of the milk; stir into soup. Cook and stir till thickened and bubbly. Add remaining milk; heat. Season to taste with salt and pepper. Makes 8 or 9 servings.

Here's beautiful soup, sparkling with vegetable jewels. Beef adds heartiness to this quick Vegetable-Burger Soup.

VEGETABLE-BEEF SOUP

½ pound ground beef
1 16-ounce can whole kernel corn, undrained
1 10¾-ounce can condensed tomato soup
1 10½-ounce can condensed beef broth
1 8-ounce can tomatoes, cut up
1 tablespoon instant minced onion
2 tablespoons butter or margarine
2 tablespoons snipped parsley

In large saucepan brown beef; drain off fat. Add remaining ingredients except parsley. Heat to boiling. Stir in parsley. Serves 4 to 6.

JIFFY MEATBALL SOUP

1 15¼-ounce can meatballs in gravy
1 16-ounce can tomatoes, cut up
1 10½-ounce can condensed onion soup
1 soup can water (1⅓ cups)
¼ cup uncooked long-grain rice

Cut meatballs in quarters. Combine all ingredients in large saucepan or Dutch oven; bring to boiling. Reduce heat; simmer, covered, for 20 minutes or till rice is tender, stirring occasionally. Makes 4 servings.

LIMA-BURGER SOUP

1 pound ground beef
1 16-ounce can lima beans, undrained
1 16-ounce can tomatoes, cut up
2 cups chopped celery
¼ cup snipped parsley
3 beef bouillon cubes
1 teaspoon salt
½ teaspoon dried thyme leaves, crushed

In large saucepan brown meat; drain off fat. Add remaining ingredients, 4 cups water, and ⅛ teaspoon pepper. Simmer, covered, 30 minutes. Remove cover; simmer 15 minutes longer. Season to taste. Makes 8 servings.

CABBAGE AND BEEF SOUP

1 pound ground beef
2 cups coarsely chopped cabbage
½ cup chopped onion
½ cup chopped celery
½ cup chopped carrot
¼ cup chopped green pepper
¼ cup snipped parsley
2 10½-ounce cans condensed beef broth
1 soup can water (1⅓ cups)
½ teaspoon salt

In large saucepan brown beef; drain off fat. Add vegetables, beef broth, water, and salt. Simmer, covered, for 15 minutes or till vegetables are tender. Makes 6 servings.

SAUSAGE AND PEA SOUP

½ pound bulk pork sausage
1 cup chopped onion
1 cup chopped celery
1 11¼-ounce can condensed green pea soup
1 10¾-ounce can condensed vegetable soup
2 soup cans water (2⅔ cups)

In large saucepan cook sausage with onion and celery till meat is browned and vegetables are tender; drain off fat. Add remaining ingredients. Heat. Makes 6 servings.

BARBECUE BEAN SOUP

½ pound ground beef
½ cup chopped onion
1 18-ounce can tomato juice
1 16-ounce can barbecue beans
1 cup water
2 ounces sharp process American cheese, shredded (½ cup)

In large saucepan cook beef with onion till meat is browned and onion is tender; drain off fat. Add tomato juice, barbecue beans, and water. Simmer, covered, for 10 minutes. Spoon into soup bowls; sprinkle each serving with cheese. Makes 6 servings.

LENTIL-BEEF SOUP

A hefty soup to take the chill out of a winter's day—

1 pound ground beef
1 16-ounce package lentils
10 cups water
1 cup chopped onion
¼ cup snipped parsley
1 tablespoon salt
⅛ teaspoon pepper
1 clove garlic, minced
1 bay leaf
1 16-ounce can tomatoes, cut up

In large saucepan or Dutch oven brown meat. Drain off excess fat. Add lentils, water, onion, parsley, salt, pepper, garlic, and bay leaf. Cover and simmer for 1½ hours, stirring occasionally. Add tomatoes; simmer, covered, 20 minutes longer. Season to taste with additional salt and pepper. Remove bay leaf before serving. Makes 10 to 12 servings.

CORN-SAUSAGE CHOWDER

Streamlined preparation is due to convenient canned and frozen foods—

1 pound bulk pork sausage
1 small onion, thinly sliced (⅓ cup)
⅓ cup chopped green pepper
• • •
2 17-ounce cans cream-style corn
1 12-ounce package loose-pack frozen hash brown potatoes
3 cups water
1 6-ounce can (⅔ cup) evaporated milk
½ teaspoon salt
4 ounces sharp process American cheese, shredded (1 cup)

In large saucepan cook sausage with onion and green pepper till meat is browned and vegetables are crisp-tender. Drain off fat. Add corn, potatoes, water, evaporated milk, and salt. Heat to boiling. Reduce heat; simmer, covered, 15 minutes or till potatoes are tender. Stir in cheese; heat till cheese melts. Serve immediately. Makes 8 to 10 servings.

GROUND BEEF CHOWDER

1 pound ground beef
2 10½-ounce cans condensed cream of chicken soup
1 soup can milk (1⅓ cups)
1 soup can water (1⅓ cups)
1 16-ounce can tomatoes, cut up
1 8½-ounce can lima beans, undrained
Dash garlic powder
Dash pepper
4 ounces sharp process American cheese, shredded (1 cup)

In large saucepan brown meat; drain off fat. Add soup; blend in milk and water. Stir in tomatoes, beans, garlic powder, and pepper. Heat just to boiling. Add shredded cheese; heat just till cheese melts. Serves 8.

MACARONI-BEEF SOUP

In large saucepan brown ½ pound ground beef, ½ cup chopped onion, and ¼ teaspoon salt till meat is browned and onion is tender; drain off fat. Add two 10¾-ounce cans condensed tomato soup; 1 cup water; 1 cup uncooked macaroni; and ¼ teaspoon dried basil leaves, crushed. Simmer, covered, 15 minutes or till macaroni is tender, stirring occasionally. Add 1½ cups milk; heat. Makes 6 servings.

BEEF AND NOODLE SOUP

1 pound ground beef
2 10½-ounce cans condensed onion soup
1 10½-ounce can condensed beef broth
3 soup cans water (4 cups)
4 ounces medium noodles, uncooked
¼ cup snipped parsley

In large saucepan or Dutch oven brown beef; drain off excess fat. Add onion soup, beef broth, water, and uncooked noodles to meat. Simmer, covered, for 15 minutes or till noodles are tender, stirring occasionally. Stir in snipped parsley just before serving. Serve in bowls. Makes 8 servings.

BARBECUE BARGAINS

Outdoor cooking, whether on the patio, at a campsite far off the beaten path, or in a picnic area, doesn't have to mean plain, unglamorous food. Preparing an outdoor feast can be fun for the whole family. Everyone can get into the act—from selecting the picnic site and fire-building to organizing the food and turning the hamburgers.

Try barbecuing on the patio. The kitchen is at hand, and so are forgotten items. But, striking out for a new location is in itself an adventure and lets the busy, everyday world pass by unnoticed. Learn the trick of assembling carry-along gear in one place so it's ready to go on the spur of the moment.

Look for lots of hamburger ideas that can be grilled over hot coals on the patio or at the campsite. And, save on cleanup by cooking complete main dishes in foil packets over a wood fire or charcoal.

Olive centers in Meatball Barbecue do double duty—add flavor and hold meatballs securely on the skewers.

Grilling on the Patio

MEATBALL BARBECUE

As shown opposite chapter introduction—

  1 beaten egg
  ¼ cup milk
  ½ cup quick-cooking rolled oats
  1 teaspoon Worcestershire sauce
  ½ teaspoon salt
  ¼ teaspoon dry mustard
    Dash pepper
1½ pounds ground beef
20 large pimiento-stuffed green
    olives
    Bottled barbecue sauce

Combine first 7 ingredients. Add beef; mix well. Shape meat around olives, forming 20 meatballs. Thread balls on skewers pushing skewer through olive. Brush with barbecue sauce. Grill over *hot* coals 8 minutes. Turn; brush with barbecue sauce. Grill 4 minutes longer or till done. Makes 5 or 6 servings.

ORIENTAL BEEF GRILL

Sweet-sour sauce on an onion-flecked burger—

    Drain one 8¾-ounce can pineapple tidbits; reserve syrup. In small saucepan combine 2 tablespoons brown sugar and 1 tablespoon cornstarch. Stir in reserved pineapple syrup, ⅓ cup water, 1 tablespoon vinegar, and 1 teaspoon soy sauce. Cook and stir over medium heat till mixture thickens and bubbles. Add drained pineapple and ½ medium green pepper cut in 2-inch strips. Return sauce to boiling. Keep warm on grill while grilling ground meat patties.

    Combine 1½ pounds ground beef, ⅓ cup thinly sliced green onion, 3 tablespoons soy sauce, and dash pepper. Shape into 6 patties. Grill over *medium* coals 6 minutes; turn and grill 6 minutes longer or till desired doneness. Serve with sauce. Makes 6 servings.

PATIO TIPS

    Don the bibbed barbecue apron and asbestos gloves and move the kitchen onto the patio, when the weather is nice. There's nothing more relaxing and appetite stimulating than eating outdoors on the patio where the conveniences of home are but a few steps away.

    Investing lots of money in elaborate barbecue equipment for the patio is not necessary since a wide range of grills is available. And, ordinary utensils can be borrowed from the kitchen.

    When outlets are handy, use electrical appliances for dining alfresco on the patio. Electric skillets can double as casserole dishes and deep-fat fryers can produce freshly fried doughnuts on the spot. Or, keep foods hot with candles, alcohol burners, or canned heat under heat-proof containers when the electrical connection is not close at hand. Chafing dishes are also good for keeping hot appetizers hot and foods such as baked beans at serving temperature.

    Another way to keep foods warm is to heat rock salt (ice cream freezing salt) in a pan on the grill or in the oven. Then nestle a bowl of food that's to be kept warm into a larger bowl filled with the heated salt. It holds the heat and keeps food warm 1 to 2 hours.

    Wrap foods in foil, such as buns or vegetables, and keep hot or heat on the edge of the grill. Foods will stay warm. Or, warm a pie, melt butter for corn on the cob, or heat a sauce in a small saucepan on the edge of the grill.

When Oriental Beef Grill sizzles over the → coals, the family will catch the aroma and come running. Prepare the sauce in the kitchen, then keep it warm on the grill while burgers cook to perfection.

APPETIZER SKEWER DOGS

1 beaten egg
2 tablespoons milk
1 cup soft bread crumbs (about 1½ slices)
2 tablespoons chopped onion
½ teaspoon salt
1 pound ground beef
16 cocktail sausages
16 dill pickle slices
1 cup catsup
¼ cup butter or margarine
¼ cup dark corn syrup
2 tablespoons vinegar

Combine first 5 ingredients and dash pepper. Add beef; mix thoroughly. Chill. Form into 16 meatballs. Thread cocktail sausages, pickles, and meatballs alternately on skewers. Grill over *medium* coals about 18 minutes, turning once or twice.

Meanwhile, combine remaining ingredients in saucepan. Simmer while kabobs cook. Brush sauce on kabobs just before removing from heat. Makes 16 appetizers.

TOTEM POLE APPETIZERS

2 tablespoons instant minced onion
¼ cup milk
1 beaten egg
½ cup finely crushed saltine cracker crumbs (14 crackers)
3 drops bottled hot pepper sauce
½ pound ground beef
16 canned whole onions
16 1-inch squares green pepper
16 pimiento-stuffed green olives
1 cup butter or margarine
1 cup extra-hot catsup

Soften minced onion in milk; combine with next 3 ingredients. Add beef; mix well. Shape into 16 logs. Thread logs lengthwise on skewers with onions, green pepper, and olives. Leave space between tidbits. Grill over *hot* coals for 8 to 10 minutes or till meat is done, turning and brushing frequently with Catsup-Butter Sauce: In saucepan heat together the butter or margarine and extra-hot catsup till butter melts. Makes 16 appetizers.

PIZZA-TOPPED BURGERS

2 pounds ground beef
1 8-ounce can pizza sauce
¼ cup grated Parmesan cheese
¼ cup finely chopped pepperoni
1 teaspoon dried oregano leaves, crushed
½ teaspoon salt
8 slices mozzarella cheese, halved
8 hamburger buns, split and toasted
¼ cup sliced pepperoni

Combine beef, ¾ *cup* of the pizza sauce, Parmesan, ¼ cup chopped pepperoni, oregano, and salt. Shape into 16 thin patties. Grill over *medium* coals 3 to 4 minutes. Turn; brush with some of the remaining pizza sauce. Top each with a half-slice of mozzarella. Grill 3 to 4 minutes longer. Serve two cheese-topped patties in each bun. Top with pepperoni slices and remaining pizza sauce. Serves 8.

POTATO CHIP BURGERS

1 pound ground beef
¼ cup chopped onion
½ teaspoon salt
1 cup crushed potato chips
4 hamburger buns, split and toasted

Combine beef, onion, salt, and dash pepper. Add potato chips; mix lightly. Shape into 4 patties, about ¾ inch thick. Grill over *medium* coals 6 minutes. Turn and grill 4 to 6 minutes or till desired doneness. Serve in split and toasted hamburger buns. Makes 4 servings.

CUMIN BURGERS

Combine 1 pound ground beef, 2 teaspoons instant minced onion, ½ teaspoon salt, ¼ teaspoon ground cumin seed, dash garlic powder, and dash pepper. Shape into 4 patties, ¾ inch thick. Grill over *medium* coals 6 minutes. Turn and grill 4 to 6 minutes or till desired doneness. Serve in 4 hamburger buns, split and toasted. Makes 4 servings.

HAWAIIAN BURGERS

Shape 1 pound ground beef into 4 patties, ½ inch thick. Drain one 8½-ounce can sliced pineapple; reserve syrup. Mix syrup with ⅓ cup bottled barbecue sauce. Pour over patties in shallow dish. Marinate 30 minutes at room temperature. Drain; reserve marinade.

Grill patties over *medium* coals 8 to 10 minutes. Turn; grill 5 minutes longer, brushing occasionally with marinade. Grill pineapple last few minutes of cooking. Place burgers on bottom halves of 4 split and toasted hamburger buns. Cover with pineapple slices and bun tops. Makes 4 servings.

JAZZY BEEFBURGERS

      ¾ cup soft bread crumbs
      ⅓ cup milk
      ¼ cup catsup
      ¼ cup finely chopped onion
      1 tablespoon prepared mustard
      1 teaspoon prepared horseradish
      1 teaspoon Worcestershire sauce
      ¾ teaspoon salt
   1½ pounds ground beef
      6 hamburger buns, split and
            toasted

Combine first 8 ingredients. Add beef; mix well. Shape into 6 patties, ½ inch thick. Grill over *medium* coals 6 minutes. Turn and grill 6 minutes or till desired doneness. Serve in toasted buns. Makes 6 servings.

DOUBLE CHEESEBURGERS

Shape 1 pound ground beef into 8 thin patties, 4 inches in diameter. Trim 4 slices sharp process American cheese and 4 slices process Swiss cheese to fit size of patties. Grill patties over *medium* coals about 3 minutes. Season with salt and pepper; turn.

Place American cheese on half the patties, Swiss cheese on remaining patties. Grill about 3 minutes, or till cheese begins to melt and meat is desired doneness. Stack Swiss cheeseburgers on top of the American cheeseburgers. Serve double burgers in 4 hamburger buns, split and toasted. Makes 4 servings.

BEEF A LA KIEV

      ¼ cup butter or margarine
      ¼ teaspoon dried thyme leaves,
            crushed
   1½ pounds ground beef
      1 teaspoon salt
      ½ cup red Burgundy
      1 tablespoon Worcestershire sauce

Blend butter with thyme. Form into 4 patties, ½ inch thick; turn out on waxed paper. Freeze till firm. Combine beef, salt, and wine; form into 4 thick burgers. Make depression in center of each, pressing down to just ½ inch from bottom. Place a piece of frozen herb-butter in each depression. Mold meat to cover butter completely.

Brush burgers with Worcestershire sauce and broil over *medium* coals 7 to 8 minutes. Turn carefully (so butter doesn't leak out) and broil 7 to 8 minutes longer. Beef will be rare next to butter. Makes 4 servings.

Scoop meat into a ½-cup measure to make uniformly-sized ¼-pound patties. Push out and mold into patty shape.

REVERSE BURGERS

1½ pounds ground beef
½ cup chili sauce
⅓ cup chopped green onion
6 slices French bread,
    cut 1 inch thick
    Butter or margarine, softened

Combine beef, chili sauce, onion, and 1 teaspoon salt; mix well. Spread *both* sides of bread with butter, then with meat mixture, using about ⅓ cup per side. Grill over *medium* coals 5 to 6 minutes; turn and grill 5 to 6 minutes longer or till meat is done. Serves 6.

LAMB AND FRANK BURGERS

⅓ cup milk
⅔ cup soft bread crumbs
¼ cup chopped green pepper
¼ cup chopped onion
1 tablespoon Worcestershire sauce
¾ teaspoon salt
1½ pounds ground lamb *or* ground
    beef
½ pound (4 to 5) frankfurters,
    diced
8 hamburger buns, split and
    toasted

Combine first 6 ingredients. Add lamb and franks; mix well. Shape into 8 patties, ½ inch thick. Grill over *medium* coals 8 to 10 minutes. Turn; grill 6 to 8 minutes or till desired doneness. Serve in buns. Makes 8 servings.

DILL PICKLE BURGERS

1½ pounds ground beef
½ cup chopped dill pickle
½ cup chopped onion
½ teaspoon salt
6 hamburger buns, split and
    toasted

Combine beef, pickle, onion, and salt; mix well. Shape into 6 patties, ½ inch thick. Grill over *medium* coals for 8 to 10 minutes; turn and grill 6 to 8 minutes or till desired doneness. Serve in buns. Makes 6 servings.

STUFFED BURGERS

1 cup packaged herb-seasoned
    stuffing mix
1 tablespoon snipped parsley
1 teaspoon lemon juice
1½ pounds ground beef
¼ cup chopped celery
¼ cup chopped onion
¼ cup milk
2 teaspoons Worcestershire sauce
½ teaspoon salt

Prepare stuffing mix according to package directions. Stir in parsley and lemon juice; set aside. Combine beef with celery, onion, milk, Worcestershire sauce, and salt.

Shape meat mixture into 12 thin patties, about 3½ inches in diameter. Spoon 2 tablespoons stuffing mixture onto *six* of the patties. Top with remaining patties and seal edges. Grill over *medium* coals 8 to 10 minutes; turn and grill 6 to 8 minutes longer or till desired doneness. Makes 6 servings.

BEER-SAUCED BURGERS

2 tablespoons chopped onion
2 tablespoons chopped green pepper
2 tablespoons butter or
    margarine, melted
½ cup catsup
2 teaspoons cornstarch
1 teaspoon Worcestershire sauce
½ cup beer
1½ pounds ground beef
1 teaspoon salt
6 hamburger buns, split
    and toasted

In small saucepan cook onion and green pepper in butter till tender but not brown. Combine catsup, cornstarch, and Worcestershire sauce. Stir into vegetables in saucepan. Add beer. Heat and stir just to boiling.

Combine beef and salt. Shape into 6 patties, ½ inch thick. Brush with beer sauce and grill over *medium* coals 8 to 10 minutes. Turn and continue grilling for 6 to 8 minutes or till desired doneness; brush occasionally with sauce. Serve in buns; spoon more hot beer sauce over. Makes 6 servings.

SAUCY MUSHROOM BURGERS

1 6-ounce can sliced mushrooms
2 tablespoons chopped green onion
2 tablespoons dry sherry
1 tablespoon all-purpose flour
¼ cup light cream
1½ pounds ground beef
6 thick slices French bread,
    toasted and buttered

Drain mushrooms, reserving liquid. In small saucepan simmer onion in reserved mushroom liquid, covered, for 5 minutes. Blend wine and flour; add to mushroom liquid. Cook and stir till mixture thickens and bubbles. Stir in mushrooms and cream; heat.

Meanwhile, shape beef into 6 oval patties, ½ inch thick. Grill over *medium* coals 8 to 10 minutes. Turn; grill 6 to 8 minutes or till desired doneness. Season with 1 teaspoon salt and dash pepper. Serve on bread; spoon mushroom sauce atop. Makes 6 servings.

VEGETABLE-BEEF ROLLS

1½ pounds ground beef
1 beaten egg
½ cup shredded carrot
¼ cup finely chopped onion
¼ cup finely chopped green pepper
¼ cup finely chopped celery
½ teaspoon salt
12 slices bacon
½ cup bottled Italian salad
    dressing

Combine beef and egg; mix well. Divide into 6 portions. On waxed paper flatten each into a 6x4-inch rectangle, ¼ inch thick. Combine carrot, onion, green pepper, celery, salt, and dash pepper; divide and pat onto meat rectangles. Roll up jelly-roll fashion. Wrap 2 slices bacon around each roll and secure with wooden picks. Place in 12x7½x2-inch baking dish. Pour salad dressing over and let stand at room temperature about 1 hour, turning occasionally to moisten all sides.

Remove from dressing; reserve dressing. Grill over *medium* coals 20 to 25 minutes; turn to grill on all sides, brushing with reserved dressing occasionally. Remove picks. Serves 6.

HAM AND HAMBURGERS

Combine 1 beaten egg, ¼ cup milk, ¼ cup fine dry bread crumbs, ¼ teaspoon salt, and dash pepper. Add 1½ pounds ground beef and one 4½-ounce can deviled ham; mix thoroughly. Shape into 8 patties, ½ inch thick. Place in 12x7½x2-inch baking dish.

Combine ½ cup red Burgundy, 2 tablespoons salad oil, and 2 tablespoons snipped parsley for marinade. Pour over patties; let stand at room temperature about 1 hour, turning once or twice. Drain; reserve marinade. Grill over *medium* coals 8 to 10 minutes, brushing occasionally with marinade. Turn; grill 6 to 8 minutes more, brushing occasionally with marinade. Serve in 8 hamburger buns, split and toasted. Makes 8 servings.

CHEESY-BACON BURGERS

2 pounds ground beef
¼ cup chopped green onion
2 teaspoons Worcestershire sauce
½ cup process cheese spread
    with bacon
8 hamburger buns, split and
    toasted

Combine beef, onion, Worcestershire sauce, and 1 teaspoon salt; shape into 8 patties, ½ inch thick. With tablespoon, make a well in center of each burger. With "well-side" down, grill burgers over *medium* coals 8 to 10 minutes. Turn; fill "well" of each burger with 1 tablespoon of the cheese spread. Grill burgers 5 to 8 minutes or till desired doneness. Serve in buns. Makes 8 servings.

PATIO MEAT LOAF

Combine 1 beaten egg; ¼ cup chili sauce; ¼ cup milk; 1 cup crushed round cheese cracker crumbs (24 crackers); and ½ envelope (¼ cup) dry onion soup mix. Add 2 pounds ground beef; mix well.

Shape meat mixture into 8x6-inch loaf, 1½ inches thick, on waxed paper. Turn into wire broiler basket. Grill over *medium* coals for 20 minutes. Turn and grill about 20 minutes longer or till desired doneness. Serves 8.

Roughing it at the Campsite

BEEF DINNER IN FOIL

- 1 pound ground beef
- 1 medium green pepper, cut in 8 rings
- 1 medium onion, sliced and separated into rings
- 3 medium carrots, cut in 3-inch strips
- 8 cherry tomatoes, halved

Shape beef into 4 patties, ¾ inch thick. Sprinkle with ¾ teaspoon salt. Tear off four 1-foot lengths of heavy foil. Center meat patty on each piece of foil. Divide vegetables among packets and layer atop meat. Draw up 4 corners of foil to center; twist securely. Bake over *slow* coals 45 to 50 minutes or till meat is done and vegetables are crisp-tender. Pass catsup if desired. Makes 4 servings.

BEEF AND BEANS IN FOIL

Combine one 16-ounce can pork and beans in tomato sauce, ¼ cup catsup, 2 tablespoons brown sugar, 1 teaspoon instant minced onion, 1 teaspoon prepared mustard, and ½ teaspoon salt. Break up 1 pound ground beef with a fork. Stir into bean mixture.

Tear off four 1-foot lengths of heavy foil. Divide bean-beef mixture in fourths and spoon onto foil. Top each mixture with a small cube of sharp process American cheese. Draw up 4 corners of foil to center; twist securely allowing room for expansion of steam. Bake over *slow* coals 45 to 50 minutes or till meat is done. Makes 4 servings.

←Beef Dinner in Foil is easy on the cleanup crew. The entire main dish is cooked in disposable heavy foil and then served on decorative throw-away plates.

COOKOUT TIPS

Play it safe when toting food to the campsite. The best rule of thumb is to keep cold food cold and hot food hot. Avoid storing and/or transporting foods between the temperatures of 50° and 120°.

To keep food cold, use a good cooler, insulated carrier, or small refrigerator and keep it out of the sun. Start out with food that has been well chilled.

Uncooked meats require special care. It's handy to shape ground meat, wrap, then chill thoroughly before placing in the cooler. An even better idea is to freeze the meat and then place it frozen in the cooler so that it can help keep the temperature low in the cooler. Uncooked meats should be taken on short excursions only or picked up daily to prevent spoilage, unless a small refrigerator or icebox is available.

Frozen foods should be solidly frozen. They help keep other foods cold in the cooler. Pack each in a plastic bag or in foil to prevent leakage.

Salads made with canned vegetables or fresh fruits travel well and can be assembled either at home or at the campsite. Toss with dressing just before serving.

If hot food is to be served—baked beans or macaroni and cheese—cook it at home, then refrigerate. Carry to the picnic in a cooler and reheat on the grill or camp stove. Or pack items separately in cooler and fix the hot foods right on the spot.

Desserts such as cream pies and picnics don't mix, even if a cooler is handy.

Cleanup is no problem if foil is used for cooking and if disposable paper and plastic items are used. If food is cooked directly on the grill, cleaning is easier when the used hot grill is removed from heat, then covered with wet paper.

CAMPERS' HASH BROWNS

1 pound bulk pork sausage
1 15½-ounce can sliced potatoes, drained and coarsely chopped
1 medium green pepper, chopped (½ cup)
1 medium onion, chopped (½ cup)
1 2-ounce jar (about 3 tablespoons) chopped canned pimiento

In large skillet brown sausage over *medium* coals, breaking up meat as it cooks. Drain off excess fat. Add potatoes, green pepper, onion, and pimiento. Cook, uncovered, for 15 to 20 minutes, turning often till potatoes are browned. Makes 4 to 6 servings.

SQUAW CORN AND SAUSAGE

½ pound bulk pork sausage
1 17-ounce can cream-style corn
1 tablespoon dried parsley flakes
4 slightly beaten eggs

In skillet brown sausage, breaking up meat as it cooks; drain off excess fat. Add corn, parsley, and dash pepper. Heat to boiling. Stir in slightly beaten eggs; cook, stirring constantly, over *medium* coals for 7 to 10 minutes or till eggs are cooked. Makes 6 servings.

CAMPSITE CHILI

2 15-ounce cans chili with beans
1 16-ounce can tomatoes, cut up
1 8-ounce can tomato sauce
1 medium onion, chopped (½ cup)
1 medium green pepper, chopped (½ cup)
1 teaspoon salt
1 7-ounce package uncooked elbow macaroni

In large kettle or Dutch oven combine chili, tomatoes, tomato sauce, onion, green pepper, and salt. Add 3½ cups water; heat to boiling over *medium* coals. Stir in macaroni and cook, covered, for 25 to 30 minutes or till macaroni is tender. Stir frequently to prevent mixture from sticking. Makes 8 to 10 servings.

CAMPFIRE SPAGHETTI

2 15-ounce cans barbecue sauce and beef
1 18-ounce can (2¼ cups) tomato juice
2 tablespoons instant minced onion
1 teaspoon dried oregano leaves, crushed
1 7-ounce package uncooked spaghetti
Parmesan cheese

Combine first 4 ingredients and 2 cups water in large kettle. Cover and bring to boiling over *medium* coals. Add uncooked spaghetti; stir to separate strands. Simmer, covered, 20 to 25 minutes or till spaghetti is tender. Stir frequently. Add more water if needed to prevent mixture from sticking. Pass Parmesan cheese, if desired. Makes 6 servings.

CAMPERS' SPANISH RICE

In large kettle cook 1 pound ground beef with 1 medium onion, chopped (½ cup), and ½ teaspoon salt over *medium* coals. Cook till meat is browned and onion is tender. Add two 15-ounce cans Spanish rice and one 16-ounce can cut green beans, drained. Bring to boiling, stirring often to prevent sticking.

Just before serving, add 2 medium tomatoes, cut in wedges; heat. Sprinkle 2 ounces sharp process American cheese, shredded (½ cup), atop. Serve from kettle. Serves 6.

HOT DOG BURGERS

1 pound ground beef
⅓ cup milk
3 frankfurters, halved lengthwise
6 frankfurter buns, split, toasted, and buttered

Combine beef, milk, ¾ teaspoon salt, and dash pepper. Shape into 6 flat rectangular burgers (frankfurter bun size). Press frank half, cut side down, into one side of each burger. Grill over *hot* coals 4 to 5 minutes. Turn; grill 4 to 5 minutes more. Serve in buns. Pass mustard or catsup, if desired. Serves 6.

SAUSAGE-APPLE WRAP

Great for brunch or supper—

>   1 pound bulk pork sausage
>   2 medium peeled apples, cored
>   and sliced (2 cups)
>   3 tablespoons sugar
>   ½ teaspoon ground cinnamon
>   1 8-ounce can whole cranberry
>   sauce

Shape sausage into 4 patties, ½ inch thick. Place each patty on a 12-inch square of heavy foil. Arrange apple slices spoke fashion atop patties. Blend sugar with cinnamon; sprinkle over apples. Spoon cranberry sauce atop. Draw up four corners of foil to center and twist to secure, allowing room for expansion of steam. Bake over *medium* coals for 20 to 25 minutes or till sausage is done and apples are tender. Makes 4 servings.

Eat like a king at the campsite with Mushroom-Bacon Burgers. Shape the man-sized patties before leaving home to

MUSHROOM-BACON BURGERS

Crisp bacon pieces give this burger extra flavor—

>   2 pounds ground beef
>   1 6-ounce can chopped mushrooms,
>   drained (1 cup)
>   8 slices bacon, crisp-cooked,
>   drained, and crumbled
>   ¼ cup sliced green onion
>   2 teaspoons Worcestershire sauce
>   1 teaspoon salt
>   8 hamburger buns, split and
>   toasted

Combine beef, mushrooms, bacon, onion, Worcestershire sauce, and salt; mix well. Shape into 8 patties, ½ inch thick. Grill over *medium* coals 8 to 10 minutes. Turn; grill 6 to 8 minutes or till desired doneness. Serve in buns with additional sliced green onion and crumbled bacon, if desired. Makes 8 servings.

eliminate on-the-spot preparation. When supper comes, grill pre-shaped patties over glowing coals or in portable gas grill.

GROUND MEAT TIPS

Versatility is the key word when thinking about ground meat. There are countless uses, and a variety of types of ground meat. Besides the staple ground beef, there is pork, veal, ham, and pork sausage. All of these can be used for the most simple or exotic dish to vary the menu daily.

Look in this chapter for tips on buying ground meat. Know what kind of beef to buy for each specific purpose and have an idea about the fat content of each kind of ground beef before buying.

Check to see which herbs are compatible with the various types of meat, then do a little experimenting on your own. It's a great way to add flavor, yet still keep the calorie count low.

And if you follow the correct freezing, storing, preparation, and cooking techniques, successful products will be the outcome.

Shape meat loaves four different ways to add variety to the meal. Just a reminder, handle the meat with a light touch.

Buying Ground Meat

Include ground meat as a part of the food budget. Whether it is ground beef, veal, lamb, or pork, ground meat is one of the most economic food buys in the meat market.

If you know the quality of ground meat to select for the dish you plan to serve, it can result in a more satisfying and delicious meal. Money can also be saved as price generally reflects the quality of the meat.

When buying ground beef, the homemaker if often confronted with a wide range of choices from which she must select. Labels such as *hamburger*, *ground beef*, *ground chuck*, *ground round*, and *ground sirloin* may only tend to confuse. Price will depend to a large extent upon the demand in a particular market of the cut from which the meat is ground.

To insure freshness, most meat is ground in the store where it is sold. In the local market the grinding operation is subject to state laws. However, the amount of fat as well as the addition of other ingredients to the meat is regulated by federal, and in some cases, special state laws. The U.S. Department of Agriculture's Consumer Marketing Service suggests that between 15 and 30 percent fat is desirable in ground meat to provide tender, juicy, and flavorful cooked meat. Too little fat produces a dry, crumbly, and flavorless cooked meat often considered less desirable.

Ground meat labeled *hamburger* may contain up to 30 percent fat (see chart, page 119). This permits the addition of beef fat beyond the fat attached to the meat before grinding. If labeled hamburger, the meat can not contain extenders such as non-fat dry milk, soybean products, cereals, or water.

Meat labeled as *ground beef* may also contain up to 30 percent fat although it is more often marketed with only 20 to 25 percent. Unlike hamburger, no additional fat may be added above that which is attached to the meat before grinding. As with hamburger, extenders can not be added. Due to the difference in fat content, hamburger when cooked usually shrinks more than ground beef. This helps to explain why hamburger is generally less expensive than ground beef.

Because shrinkage is relatively high and less tender meat is used, hamburger and ground beef are best suited for casseroles, skillets, soups, and similar dishes which include other ingredients. If used alone, as in patties, shrinkage is more noticeable.

Ground chuck, ground from the chuck wholesale cut, contains only 15 to 25 percent fat. It is ideal for patties as shrinkage is not too great, yet it contains enough fat to provide a juicy, flavorful burger. Since it is ground from a more popular cut, the price is usually higher than either hamburger or ground beef.

Meat ground from round steak is marketed as *ground round*. It contains only about 11 percent fat giving a somewhat dry and compact patty unless other ingredients are added for moistness. Ground from a popular cut, it is often priced higher than ground chuck.

Ground sirloin, ground from the high-priced sirloin steak, is the most expensive of the ground meats. As a result of its fine flavor, it makes an excellent burger but is generally considered too expensive to be purchased just for the serving of hamburgers.

Color is a helpful guide to identifying the different kinds of ground meat (see page 116). Meat ground from the beef carcass varies from pale red to bright red (in meat ring), ground lamb ranges from pinkish red to deep red (in glass loaf dish), ground pork is grayish pink (in metal baking pan), and ground veal appears light pink (in muffin pan). Color will also vary depending upon freshness and handling after grinding. Meat tends to brighten with exposure to air.

The quantity of meat purchased will depend primarily upon family size and type of storage available. Unless ground meat can be properly stored and used before it begins to decline in quality, money is not really saved even though a larger quantity is purchased at a lower price. Thus, consider menu plans as well as storage available before buying.

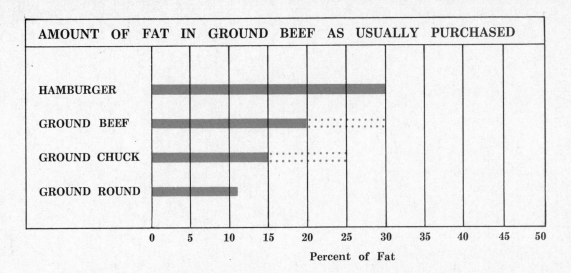

AMOUNT OF FAT IN GROUND BEEF AS USUALLY PURCHASED

Percent of Fat

CALORIES TO COUNT

Ground meat is generally ground from less tender cuts of meat. However, this does not affect its nutritional value. Tender and less tender cuts of meat contain about the same amount of protein, vitamins, and minerals. Consequently, it is one of the most economical as well as nutritional buys.

The caloric value will depend upon the amount of fat in the meat before grinding as well as the amount added. But, fat should not be considered synonymous with calories as it contributes to flavor and juiciness. For those counting calories or on low-fat diets, meat relatively low in fat, such as round steak, is best for grinding. If calories aren't crucial, have a little additional fat ground with the meat for more juicy, flavorful meat. Or, select from the meat counter a cut of meat with more fat attached for grinding.

The method of cooking determines to a degree the caloric count of the meat dish. If fat is added, as in panfrying or deep fat frying, the total number of calories soars. If meat is broiled or panbroiled, however, some of the fat is lost since the fat is drained off; thus, the number of calories is reduced.

If a specific calorie count is necessary, check the calorie chart to compute the day's totals. Remember though, casseroles and skillets include other ingredients which increase the caloric value of the meat dish.

HERBS TO USE

Heighten the flavor of ground meat with the addition of herbs and spices. By using just the right seasoning, an acceptable food is transformed into a mouth-watering dish. Experiment with different seasonings. Smaller amounts are needed when combined with other seasonings. Starting with $\frac{1}{4}$ teaspoon dried herb for every 4 servings, increase the amount until desired flavor level is reached.

To use dried herb leaves, crush the leaves between the fingers before combining with other ingredients. If available, use fresh herbs rather than dried. Since they are not as concentrated as dried, add 3 times the amount and snip, rather than crush.

Begin with seasonings popular with the family; then, venture into new flavor combinations. Some familiar seasonings often added to beef include chili powder, garlic, mustard, and oregano. For a change of pace, add basil, cumin, curry, dill, marjoram, savory, or thyme. Accent veal with basil, curry, ginger, mace, marjoram, mustard, sage, or savory. Lamb is a natural with mint, oregano, rosemary, savory, or thyme. Try blending the subtle flavor of pork with clove, ginger, garlic, mustard, oregano, sage, or thyme. Pair ham with allspice, cinnamon, clove, ginger, or mustard. Sausage may not need additional seasoning, but if mildly seasoned, flavor with garlic, oregano, sage, or thyme.

Freeze Basic Ground Beef in 2-cup portions. To use, thaw in saucepan over low heat according to recipe directions.

To freeze meatballs, shape meat on cookie sheet and place in freezer. When frozen, transfer balls to plastic bag and seal.

To freeze meat patties, wrap each patty in clear plastic wrap or waxed paper. Seal in round container or plastic bag.

Freezing and Storing

The versatility of ground meat makes it an excellent food to have on hand for quick meals or unexpected dinner guests. Its keeping quality in comparison to other foods, however, is quite short unless properly wrapped and refrigerated. Ground meat is more perishable than steaks, roasts, or chops since it has been ground, thus exposing more of the surface area of the meat to the air. Consequently, unless a freezer is available, only the amount of ground meat which can be used within 2 days should be purchased at one time.

To insure maximum freshness and quality of ground meat as it is purchased, remove store wrappings and rewrap loosely with waxed paper immediately after purchasing. Store in the coldest part of the refrigerator and use within 2 days. When a freezer is available, storage time for ground meat may be lengthened up to 2 to 3 months. Wrap tightly in moisture-vaporproof material such as freezer paper or plastic bags. Seal; label with the name of contents, date, and amount. Freeze at 0° or below.

Ground meat readily lends itself to pre-preparation before freezing. This in turn can reduce or eliminate thawing time. Pre-shaping into meatballs or patties can shorten total meal preparation time as well as eliminate the problem of leftovers. Only the number of meatballs or patties needed for each meal need to be removed from the freezer.

Ground meat may also be cooked ahead as in Basic Ground Beef (see page 87), frozen in small portions, and then used directly from the freezer. Such a mixture lends itself to quick skillet meals, jiffy meat sauces, or speedy barbecue mixtures for sandwiches. If ground meat is frozen in individual or family-sized portions, it need not be thawed before cooking although cooking time should be lengthened slightly to allow for thawing.

Preparation Pointers

Simplify the mixing of meat loaf by using only one bowl. Blend dry ingredients with egg and liquid before adding meat.

Ground meat, as purchased, is often quite compact due to the method of packaging. As a result, combining the meat with other ingredients presents a special problem when making meat loaf. For a well-mixed loaf, combine the dry extender (such as bread crumbs or cereal) with the liquid ingredients. This insures that the dry ingredients are moistened. Then stir in the chopped vegetables (such as onion or green pepper) and seasonings before adding the meat. Thus, a more uniform mixture of ingredients is possible. Handle the meat lightly and only as much as necessary to mix ingredients thoroughly. Overmixing tends to make a more compact loaf.

Meat loaves will vary in juiciness depending upon the percent of fat in the meat. The addition of liquid and dry ingredients tends to make the loaf juicier and less compact. A very tender meat loaf may be difficult to remove from the pan, while a less tender and more compact loaf will be easier to slice and less likely to crumble.

A combination of meats in a meat loaf is sometimes used to give a different flavor or texture. Again, thorough mixing is a must for a uniform loaf. Finely chopped bacon or bulk pork sausage may be added to very lean meat to make the loaf moist.

To prepare juicy, tender hamburgers, handle the meat as little as possible. Patties may be panbroiled in a skillet, pouring off fat as it accumulates; cooked in a preheated skillet in which salt has been sprinkled to reduce sticking; or broiled (see page 88). The method of cooking will most often be determined by family preference, as all of the methods, if done correctly, will produce a flavorful hamburger. When cooking, avoid flattening patties with a spatula as many of the juices will be lost. Learn to judge the amount of cooking time needed for the degree of doneness desired. Just as with meat loaves, patties will be dry and lack flavor if overcooked.

When browning ground meat, break up meat with a potato masher or fork for even browning. Drain off fat, if desired.

To brown evenly and keep meatballs round, shake skillet back and forth over heat, browning only a few at a time.

Know How to Shape Meat

For ground meat products that are juicy and light, the trick is to handle the meat as little as possible. Too much handling gives ground meat a compact texture. This is not desirable in meat loaves, patties, or meatballs.

One of the most popular ways of shaping ground meat is into a meat loaf. Changing the shape of the loaf is a simple way to vary meat loaves without altering the ingredients in the recipe, although baking time may need to be changed. Check the picture opposite the chapter introduction for some of the following ideas. If a meat loaf with lots of outside crust is what the family prefers, shape the meat mixture into a loaf in a shallow baking pan. Bake, uncovered, for a slightly shorter time than for loaves shaped in a loaf pan or dish. For those who prefer less outside crust on the meat loaf, lightly pat the mixture into a regular loaf pan or dish. And for a decorative touch, make grooves in the top of the loaf. Use the handle of a wooden spoon and press gently into the meat, making slight indentations. Fill with sauce, if desired.

For a change, how about patting the meat loaf mixture gently into a ring mold and then turning it out onto a shallow baking pan. Or, if a less crusty loaf is desired, bake it in an oven-going aluminum mold. The center of the baked ring loaf can then be used for serving vegetables, such as peas, potatoes, or carrots. Or, it can be trimmed with parsley sprigs and served handsomely for company dinners. It is also attractive filled with sauce.

How about individual servings of meat loaf? It's simple to do. Just pat meat mixture into muffin pans. This cuts down on baking time considerably and makes shorter work out of dinner preparation.

←Pat ground meat mixture into a rectangle on waxed paper and use the paper to aid in rolling up Filled Beef Roll.

Another way to use ground meat is to shape it into meatballs. To make even-sized meatballs, pat the meat mixture gently into a rectangle on waxed paper, then cut into even squares. Roll each square into a ball. When shaping meatballs, try wetting hands with cold water, then roll between cupped hands. This helps keep the meat from sticking to the hands and balls can be formed with little if any pressure. Another trick is to chill the ground meat mixture in the refrigerator before forming it into meatballs.

The most familiar way to shape ground meat is into patties. When shaping meat patties, pat the meat mixture gently and evenly into rounds. Make them as thick at the edges as in the center for even cooking. There are several ways to shape evenly-sized patties. Use a ⅓- or ½-cup measure as a quantity guide. Turn out of cup and gently form into patties. Or, pat the meat between two large sheets of waxed paper till it is ½ or ¾ inch thick. Cut burgers with a jumbo cookie cutter. Or, gently form ground meat into a roll 3 inches thick on a piece of waxed paper. Cut into ½- to ¾-inch slices.

Waxed paper and foil come in handy when shaping meat, especially when making meat rolls and stuffed meat loaves. It's also useful for transferring large pieces of uncooked ground meat when a utensil is not large enough to lift the meat.

For meat rolls, pat meat mixture onto waxed paper into the specified size. Spoon filling evenly over meat leaving a margin around the edge so filling won't spill out. Using the waxed paper as a guide, pick up adjacent corners of the paper along one edge of the meat and pull straight up and over, allowing meat to roll over filling. Seal side seam and ends by pressing meat together. The meat roll can then be picked up with the waxed paper and transferred to a baking pan. Then, just slip the paper out from under the meat roll.

INDEX
A-B

124